10659680

Audrey Albert

The **Dog** with the

Chip in His **Neck**

Books by Andrei Codrescu

(Andrei
Codrescu)

The **Dog** with the
Chip in His **Neck**

Essays from **NPR** and Elsewhere

ST. MARTIN'S PRESS ❦ NEW YORK

THE DOG WITH THE CHIP IN HIS NECK. Copyright © 1996 by Andrei Codrescu. All rights reserved. Printed in the United States of America. No
part of this book may be used or reproduced in any manner whatsoever
without written permission except in the case of brief quotations em-
bodied in critical articles or reviews. For information, address St. Martin's Press, 175 Fifth Avenue, New York, N.Y. 10010.

Design by Songhee Kim

Copyright acknowledgments for previously published material are on
page 269–270.

Library of Congress Cataloging-in-Publication Data

Codrescu, Andrei.
    The dog with the chip in his neck : essays from NPR and
elsewhere
  / Andrei Codrescu.
      p.   cm.
    ISBN 0-312-14316-8
    I. National Public Radio (U.S.)   II. Title.
  PS3553.O3D6   1996
  814'.54–dc20   96-6428
                                                             CIP

First Edition: August 1996

10   9   8   7   6   5   4   3   2   1

COnteNts

Part 2
The Dog with the Chip in His Neck

Part 3
Swimming Between Languages

Part 4
The Meat in Motion

INtroDuction: I'll Say

The writings collected here are the sleepless notices of an obsolete idealist. Happily, a useful cynic has seen fit to simultaneously check the excesses. At the same time, no two human dispositions can stem the fatal leakage of the world into a non-verbal, ex-thoughtful, alibi-free sewer drain.

My editor has done well to characterize these lucubrations as a late chapter in a "novel of ideas." Just like characters in a novel, ideas rush blithely to their ends. Some novelists follow their characters past their deaths into the afterworld and, on a few occasions, I went right after them into cyberspace like a Mac Orpheus. Cerberus, the dog with the chip in his neck, was snoozing. Imagine my surprise when I found Hades vacant, its pits full of blah-blah, no one suffering.

Warnings of soul loss were once a constant feature of empathic journalism. Before the crash-landing of Communist ideology even economics was fraught with strands of (fragile) morality. In the West, psychology held hands with religious ideas often enough to make it seem that a higher purpose attended us, even if it was only a shred of social sensitivity. Those things are gone now. The market is "free," which is to say savage. Psychology has divorced higher purpose and married Prozac. Religion has become the province of fundamentalists, people whose rock-hard faith is only matched by their bonehead politics. And in the social arena, we are urged by the Gingrich Party to abandon all face-to-face intercourse and link up by laptop. Which means, death to the cities, they are damned anyway.

Our time is remarkable for the ferocity of change. Even ten years ago things stayed still long enough to be noted and addressed. We no longer have that luxury. As soon as we open our mouth to speak the ostensible objects move out of reach. The future, which used to be ahead of us, is now mostly past. At the center of New Orleans stands a two-thirds-finished building that had been intended for a mega-casino, the solution, it was believed, to our economic future. The ruins of that future are now as plain as the Roman Forum's. A future without a history is but one of the paradoxes that haunt these essays. The other is that public discourse is now as devoid of permanence as the future past. An enormous inflation of speech agitates the airwaves and the word-gorged cyberspace.

I would like these pieces to serve as a combative form of silence. Some of them are radio essays from NPR, 1994–96, while others address revolution, food, America, sex, Romania, and language—my characters. Controversy has attended some of these creatures after they became public. The Romanian government had a fit when I laid the charge of fascism at its door at the time they were in Washington, begging for favors. They haven't become any less fascist since. Christian fundamentalists have reserved a special place in Hell for me, at the center, I believe, of the Lake of Fire. Their ire was aroused by the obvious: they are laughable. Others have objected to the bluntness of some of my bludgeoning. I'll use an icepick next time. But note, dear Reader, the exuberant enticements in some of these writings. There is dance music here and there, trying to drown out the funeral marches.

Andrei Codrescu
New Orleans
January 19, 1996

America **Right** and **Wrong**

Part 1

My House in the Sky

I came to America on a chartered plane full of immigrants who started chanting, "America! America!" when the coastline of Nova Scotia slid into view. The morning sun had gold-leafed the scalloped shore like a Christmas present. The church steeples of New England glinted from the snow, bespeaking an orderly world, still tied by tradition to the Europe we had left behind. Nonetheless, even from this height there was already something more open, more fearless, and more prosperous about this coastline, its villages and fields. They were not surrounded by fortifications, they did not look suspiciously outward over gun emplacements. Centuries of immigrants had preceded me but those huddled masses arriving by ship had never been presented with such a glorious package. Inside that package was my new home, though I didn't yet know which one it was.

The slight kinship with the Old World evaporated soon enough. The pilot banked his big bird over New York so that the view became indelible. The Statue of Liberty came into view, slipping quite easily into the space already reserved for her in our minds. We had seen her so many times in pictures, she had a home already there, behind our eyes. The towers of Manhattan thrust into the cloudless blue sky, proclaiming their resolute break with old Europe. New York was tall and erect where the cities of Europe had lain lazily, hugging the shores. America proclaimed its vigor and energy with the exclamation points of her towers. The canyons between were filled with the turbulent rage of torrents of cars, and millions of windows sparkled in the sun.

I must have flown into New York dozens of times from every direction since then but I still get that slight chill of wonder at its unapologetic pride. Manhattan's towers are emblematic of this "American century," the century of the industrial might that has now become the Age of Information. The raw muscle and imagination of immigrants first made a powerful impression here. I was shocked by one raw image after another. I saw a fleet of buses at rest, sleek like plump seals, ready to stream into the dynamic of the great city. From the top of the World Trade Tower I saw the electric nerves of the metropolis, glowing with the flush of material well-being. No matter what gloomy thoughts I subsequently had in the city where I ended up living for two years, these first images revive in me that new feeling of fearless liberty. New York City is seen best from the air because its citizens already live in the air and the city tends continually upward. "Going up" and "moving up" are true American metaphors, enclosing the ever-upward urge that finds its purest embodiment in the city of Walt Whitman, the poet who proudly called himself "the son of Mannahatta."

"The central fact of man in North America is SPACE," wrote the poet Charles Olson, speaking of the insight of an earlier American and fellow New Englander, Herman Melville. In truth, space, in its larger and generous amplitude, does not begin until one begins to head north and west. After a stop at Kennedy Airport, the refugee plane took off for Detroit where the Jewish Refugee Organization (HIAS) was prepared to welcome yet another passel of hopeful souls to America's generous vastness. We passed over rivers festooned with both working and idle industrial giants, and large farms covered with comforters of deep snow under which the world's bounty of grain slept in expectation of spring. Detroit itself came into view carrying the grime of the industrial age like a heavy mantle. The Rouge River was frozen, but the River Rouge plant wrote in the sky with smoke a message that must have lifted the spirits of hundreds of thousands of Eastern Europeans since early in the century: "There is work! The engines are humming!" Or so it seemed to me, in those almost innocent days of the midsixties before the oil embargo, inflation, and Japanese cars.

The views of the Midwest bespoke both the story of that innocence and the subsequent history. The Great Lakes, these inland seas, held mighty ships full of the riches of the land-seas that surrounded them. The patterns of wheat, corn, sunflower, mustard, soy, alfalfa were firmly drawn. I could easily see from the air the plenitude that had focused the hunger of the world. In the 1903 novel *The Pit*, by Frank Norris, a madman decides to corner the midwestern wheat market, gambling on a meager harvest. The repercussions are widespread: there is famine in Europe and distress elsewhere. But the earth, resplendent in her independence and resentful of selfishness, brings forth an abundant crop. The arrogant trader is buried under waves and waves of wheat. From the air, I could see all the relationships at once: that of farmer to the land, of land to harvest, of harvest to boundary, and above all, that humility is the proper response to the land. And after that, joy.

Later I flew everywhere and the map moved within.

The bold skyline of Chicago sprawls like the signature of a bank guarantor for the land's wealth. The buildings of Chicago display no false modesty as they mingle the efficacy of commercial purpose with the daring of modern architecture. The hypocritical scruples of the Old World, which deemed its opera houses more refined than its banks, are gone here. From the air, Chicago displays both its shiny railways like a workman's veins, and the ostentatiously fancy dress of its transparent towers. Chicago too aims to live in the air and move up but, unlike New York, it is more firmly connected to the commodities that fuel its growth. The penthouses of the tall towers still smell of loam and crushed grain: they share a spirit with the silos that surround them in the darkness of the countryside.

America's industry is most visible in the Midwest, but the earlier shapes and aims of the land have not been completely buried by the efforts of modern Americans. In Ohio the great Serpent Mound is witness to an Amerindian civilization of which little is known beyond the massive monuments of mounds that stretch from Ohio to Mississippi. Even the history of the westward migration is still visible in the form of scars left by covered wagons on the Oregon Trail.

From a car, the intimacy of each bend in the road is reassuring. You can stop and take the measure of the place, revel in its particulars. Each letter or syllable of the topography stands alone, its relation to others not very clear. From the air, the patterns of nature and the works of man mingle to make sentences, phrases, pages. I often see a writing.

Cities, of course, write in lights. The quiet towns write an electric but orderly story, looking out of their windows with the disciplined glow of work and self-control. After the ten or eleven o'clock news, their eyes blink shut at once, leaving only their traffic lights and control towers to keep watch over them. Other cities, chief among them Las Vegas, write a different story with unleashed and parti-colored neon. Las Vegas, like Coney Island at night, sends up messages of guilt-free joy that look like whirling loops, spinning rings, geysers. America spends a staggering quantity of electricity to keep her cities illuminated at night. And yet, for all that expense and energy, I have often looked from the window of a plane at night and thought how, for the most part, North America is dark. The illuminated oases of the cities are only little dots on the great map of the continent. North America, despite the cries of alarm raised by those panicked by human civilization, is still mostly wood, mountain, desert, farm, and water.

Deciphering the various messages of the American landscape requires an eclectic knowledge, but it also involves fancy and imagination: one joins the clouds in reading the sometimes playful, sometimes painful script. Looking up at the clouds is very much like looking down from them. When my children were young, we used to lie in the grass and see everything we ever knew or could think of by looking at the clouds. The earth spinned with us and we with it and the stories of the sky were infinite. It isn't much different, looking down on the enigmatic and suggestion-rich formations of the Southwest, to see our most intimate images reflected there. The reach and limitations of the human imagination become quickly evident above the Grand Canyon, for instance.

Standing at Hopi Point on the south rim of the Grand Canyon at sunset I knew for certain that the earth was greater than all of men's works. I knew also, beyond a shadow of doubt, that I preferred America to the Europe I had left behind. "The poetry of earth is never dead," wrote John Keats, but in Europe the earth had been tamed, the wilderness made sensible. Here was the romantic vision of Keats and the dreamscape of Coleridge's "caverns measureless to man." The complex grandeur of what lay beneath was an argument without rebuttal. The mountains and buttes were awash in color. Layers of mineral and fossil rock told a timeless geological story. The peaks and valleys below had their own weather. The human story, told in rock painting, carving, and artifact, began with the Archaic People of 2500 B.C., on to the Anasazi of 1100 A.D., through the Havasupai and Hopis in the 1800s, and the Navajos in the 1900s. Here was space, revealed from within, a gift from mother earth to me. Francisco Vásquez de Coronado, the first white man to have seen the canyon in 1540, thought that he had found the Seven Cities of Gold. Subsequently, men whose imaginations failed them, named the mountains and formations of the Grand Canyon after castles, temples, and gods of the Old World. Below me lay Isis, Buddha, Diva, Brahma, and Zoroaster, mountains named after the most awesome creations of the mystic imagination. This heroic nomenclature fails to persuade because the landscape is irreducibly itself, a masterwork of the Colorado River and of the sky. I could see how other metaphors might proceed from it, but not the other way around. This was a source.

Walt Whitman wrote, "Something startles me where I thought I was safest." The North American landscape often mocks our human-measured notion of safety and scale. Early English travelers did not like America. It was too big and unmanageable. To British writer Frances Trollope, Niagara Falls was "an accompaniment to conversation," while the same body of water elicited this from Oscar Wilde: "The sight of the stupendous waterfall must be one of the first, if not the keenest, disappointments in American married life." All the effort to civilize, miniaturize, and bring the world inside comes to naught in America. Many early explorers left their bones in the desert or in the swift waters of the Colorado. I try to imagine what it must have been like to see the Grand Canyon for the first time like Coronado, or to behold the Mississippi like Hernando de Soto. For them, it must have been a lot like being airborne. The vistas must have spoken to them on a planetary scale. What they said was not easily decipherable. The Hopi Indians, who were at the canyon first, read poetry in what lay below: "The song resounds back from our Creator with joy, / and we of the earth repeat it to our Creator."

After emigrating to Detroit in 1966 I did not stay put long. The siren call of the North American continent combined with the adventurous spirit of the age drove me west. I followed the classic route of the western migrant, only I traveled by bus and car not by air. I learned my new country mile by mile of endless ribbon of road, city by city. From New York to San Francisco, through prairie, mountains, and deserts, I learned to appreciate her awesome dimensions. The spirits of the land grew stronger the farther west I traveled. I shared my new home with the spirits that inhabited the rocks and the bottoms of vanished seas long before I came. Driving America by car I tasted the density of her roots. Had I walked I would have distinguished the even finer particulars of that density, but I wouldn't have been able to cover very much. America was meant to be seen by air: the Native Americans esteemed the eagle above all because of its ability to soar and encompass.

Perspective is at the source of all knowledge. What we see depends on where we stand. Not very long ago, human beings could not see very much. I remember staring in wonder at fifteenth-century aerial views of Sibiu, my medieval hometown in Romania. These intricate drawings had been composed from the top of the highest hill overlooking the city. Proceeding from the church in the central square, the town fanned out concentrically to the fortified wall that surrounded it. Beyond the wall there was nothing as lofty to be seen. I loved finding my house (built in 1456) in those drawings.

Later, I flew in a glider over the town and found my house again, only this time it was part of an even larger shape because I saw also the foothills that hugged the city—which had expanded far beyond its medieval walls—and the snowcapped mountains that hugged the hills. I now saw more than my grandfather, who had seen our world from his horse, or my father, who'd driven it in a car. For them, the shapes of the unknown landscapes ahead held dangers proportional to the distances they could cover. Everything beyond the capacity of their transport was fraught with peril, it belonged to the hostile outside, the place that was not home.

In the spaces of North America, the sense of peril does not come from rival cities over the hill but from the loneliness of one's habitation. With the exception of those few star bursts of cities, the North American night is dark, its dimensions still inviolate. Finding one's home from the air in such immensity has both pathos and poetry.

I was jotting these notes in the air, on the approach to the Philadelphia airport, when I heard a breathless young girl behind me tell her mother: "Look, Mom, there is our house!"

The pilot was banking the plane knowingly over the snowy jigsaw puzzle below. It was February and a snowstorm had just left the area. I saw the ice on the Susquehanna, the reactor of a nuclear plant with the white puff of steam over it like a fat dragon, an accordion-like subdivision, a white football field. Somewhere in there was the little girl's house.

"There, Mom!" she said, frustration building in her voice because the mother, not as quick as her daughter, hadn't spotted it yet.

Perhaps the child was already endowed with a greater capacity for seeing more and in greater detail than her mother. She was at home in the air, more so than her elders, who came of age when flight was still a rarity.

I now live in New Orleans, near the mouth of the Mississippi River. When you fly over the Mississippi floodplain between the river and Lake Pontchartrain into the port of New Orleans, the little patches of land that float on the water look like afterthoughts. It doesn't seem as if people could live on these tiny, tufted islands. But, in fact, the land is a first thought, not an afterthought. The land is a first thought of the big river as it moves the soil of the plains into the Gulf of Mexico. Consequently, everything that lives here, including myself, is the aftermath of the river's first thought.

In this ecoregion of the Messachebe (the Choctaw Indians' name for the Mississippi) water is our medium. We live in it, we talk of it, we are thought by it, we see the world through it. The Mississippi, since its very first recorded sighting by de Soto in 1542, has been giving us a flood of stories exceeded only by the volume of its waters. One might say, paraphrasing Herodotus, that American literature is a gift of the Mississippi. But then so is Louisiana, where I live now. Yet this magnificent river, which runs through the imaginations of all the boys in the world, is not one of us. In fact, it is mad at us.

The flood of 1993, the largest in the river's recorded history, also flooded our national consciousness. Talk of the river has risen steadily past the estimates of financial damage to unsettling questions about the nature of our relationship with this "strong brown god," as T. S. Eliot called it. Mark Twain, who learned the book of the river by heart, said so right from the start in *Life on the Mississippi:* "Ten thousand river commissions, with the mines of the world at their back, cannot tame that lawless stream, cannot curb it or confine it, cannot say to it, 'Go here,' or 'Go there,' and make it obey; cannot save a shore which it has sentenced; cannot bar its path with an obstruction which it will not tear down, dance over and laugh at." No one listened. Since 1927, the Army Corps of Engineers has built, dredged, and dug $25 billion worth of levees, dams, and channels along the Mississippi and its tributaries. We spend $2 billion each year for flood damage. There are twenty locks and dams on the river above Hannibal, Missouri, Twain's boyhood town.

Between the hilltop of the cartographer and the orbit of the spaceman there are countless heights from which to see the world. They all yield a different knowledge, but they all have in common the little girl's exclamation: "Look, Mom, there is our house!" Paradoxically, the higher we get and the more we see, the more important our specific speck of dirt becomes. It is the search for our specificity in the larger scheme of things that inspires flight. What is revealed is the pattern wherein we dwell, the coherence of the physical body.

To see from the air is to see philosophically because you see the patterns. But what is the correct height from which to see America? How high do you have to be to see the nation? What is the height of being able to see not just geographically but politically, socially, morally?

A few years ago, the artist Christo, together with an air force general, a sheep farmer, and the marine biologist Peter Warshall, flew over part of Northern California to survey the site for Christo's sculpture *The Running Fence*. This was the first time that these people, each one with a special interest in one aspect of the land, had seen it from the point of view of others. The general, whose base covered a good area, had never seen it as the home of plants, animals, marine life-forms, grazing ground, a canvas for art. The sheep farmer, who had seen it only as a grazing ground, was astonished to see all its other faces. Peter, who had seen only the life-forms in the water hugging the coast, saw a different kind of diversity. But it was Christo, the artist, who brought them all together by means of a daring, imaginary construct. When the white nylon fence was finally constructed, it sliced through the hills like a white wing, or a sail, lifting the landscape as if it were airborne. During the time *The Running Fence* fluttered there in the wind, everyone in the area participated in a passionate debate about the place that they had—until that time—inhabited blindly. Seeing one's home from the air has the same effect: it brings home the realization that one's place on earth is multifaceted, complex, and beautiful.

My aerial views have been almost exclusively from the windows of commercial airliners. At thirty thousand feet, to the naked eye, the landscape yields only its major structures. Snowy alpine ridges and inland seas seem quite friendly. There is no hint of their difficulty, desolation, or severity. But each height reveals a specific mystery. To the maker of weather maps from images beamed down by satellites, patterns have precise meanings. To the nonspecialist, such as myself, the wealth of forms speaks of abstraction and symmetry. I see shapes that look like alien landing pads, and the ridges, mountaintops, rivers are to me the bones, tops, and veins of the earth. It is perhaps a testimony to the inability of humans to transcend themselves that the body becomes the measure of everything we see. Still, it is true: when I look at the earth below, I see a body that is partly mine.

Until I Got Here— America Boring

Do you know how boring this country was before I got here? I'm not saying that I made it personally less boring, only that my arrival and the assault on boredom were synchronous. In 1966 in Detroit, Michigan, for instance, if one had a craving for anything except mashed potatoes and roast beef, there were precious few places to go: Greektown, which had Greek food, Hamtramck, which had Polish food, and the Ho Ho Inn, a Cantonese Chinese restaurant where everything tasted like rasberry jam and mustard (which also coated the menu).

Even New York in those days, wasn't the ethnic smorgasbord it is today. Chinese did mean mostly Cantonese, and the ethnic neighborhoods did dish out blintzes and Cuban sandwiches, but for the most part mashed potatoes and gravy ruled. Most of America rested on a bedrock of bland and that was how most people were, too. Everybody was nice and white, for the most part, and geography wasn't anybody's forte. Nobody'd heard of Romania, where I had come from, but they were willing to give it the benefit of the doubt. If I hankered for spice in Detroit I had to go to Twelfth Street, in the ghetto, to get ribs and listen to music in "blind pigs," illegal joints that stayed open past midnight. Gay people met in bars with parrots on the sign and everybody with the least bit of difference in them was afraid of the FBI.

Happily, this state of affairs changed rather suddenly when there was an invasion of color and sound in 1966 and the mental and physical gates of America swung open briefly, letting in some happiness and a whole lot of exotics from Latin America, to be followed, in the coming years by spicier and more vividly hued ones from Asia and Africa. I only mention this because at this moment the same gates seem to be in danger of being shut by bigots in California and everywhere else. Simple-minded souls who want to go back to the safety of their 1950s doo-wop mashed potatoes are fixing to take away our hot sauce. Don't let them, folks. Trust me: boredom is hell.

Roll On, Big River!

My world is made of water, a fact that makes me feel both transitory and humble. It's an ambiguous blessing, best expressed on the grave of John Keats in Rome: "Here lies a young English poet who in the bitterness of his heart at the maliciousness of his enemies, desired these words to be writ on his tomb: 'Here lies one whose name was writ on water.' " John Keats was an English Romantic for whom water was the medium of oblivion. He understood with melancholy precision the awesome power of our original matrix. Americans, however, are optimists. We are a nation of engineers, not poets, and are baffled when nature mocks our engineering.

When I was a boy growing up in the mountains of Romania I read *Life on the Mississippi* by Mark Twain and got chills of wonder spelling the name of the mighty river. I suffered alongside the young pilot the arduous task of learning every bend, every tree, every comma, colon, and dash in the "book" of the river. I grew dreamy and daring with the inexhaustible stories spawned by the river.

The town of Hannibal, population 18,004, was waiting for the river to crest at thirty-two feet on July 11, 1993, when I pulled in. It was the middle of the night and I felt as if I had been riding on water all the way from St. Louis. The slick, black stretch limo provided by the producers of "Nightline," for whom I was doing a story, glided like a hearse on the deserted road. I felt the presence of the river on all sides as my long coffin advanced noiselessly to the heart of the flood. I rolled down the window and the smell of the water rushed in, a thick, muddy smell heavy with summer. Everything felt swollen, outsized. The half-moon moving in and out of the clouds was puffed up like a wineskin. Its light fell now and then on billboards touting the WORLD FAMOUS MARK TWAIN CAVE, SAWYER'S CREEK AMUSEMENT PARK, CLEMENS LANDING, MARK TWAIN'S COUNTRY AND MUSIC SHOW, PUDD'NHEAD'S CRAFTS AND ANTIQUES. I felt quite absurd, a late twentieth-century fleck of dust inside an oversized container, going to gather news of water in a tourist trap. I could hear Mark Twain's mocking, knowing laugh as he surveyed these simulacra of his image. The river, he knew, didn't care. It was going to rise and rise until it had enough, then it would draw back leaving behind swarms of pests, stranded snakes, broken hearts, bankrupt farms, and a thousand stories. And, of course, tons of sand in sandbags or out of them that no one I talked to knew what to do with after the flood. I slept uneasily for a few hours, feeling the water lapping at my bed.

In the early morning, the lobby of the Holiday Inn in Hannibal was swarming with National Guardsmen who were there to help the town's citizens and the Army Corps raise the levee. They were also there in case evacuation orders came and they were needed to patrol the Mark Twain industry in downtown Hannibal from looters.

"Haven't seen these many uniforms since Somalia," my producer said. Indeed. There was that air of occupation familiar to me, which always gives me the creeps. I knew what the good guardsmen were there for, but I grew up seeing enough uniforms to give me a permanent phobia. Last time *I* had seen these many National Guard men was in Detroit during the riots of 1967. They were armed then and had orders to shoot.

I caught some of their talk. "I saw a house floating by right near Route 79," and "This guy was running in a rising creek with a keg of beer over his head." "Three kids who were fishing saved a man sinking in his car." "People are taking turns sleeping, watching for the flood."

Such stories would doubtless form the body of legend in the future. On the levee, which had been raised two feet from thirty-three to thirty-five, spectators were already gathering. It was a somber crowd, mostly families with children. They gazed over the wide waters, at the half-buried silos, at the closed bridge flooded at Quincy on the Illinois side. A street sign that said STOP stuck out of the river incongruously, giving new meaning to the word *traffic*. I saw only a few logs and a barrel go by. I remembered Twain's story of the "haunted barr'l," a supernatural object that dogged the crew of a boat until one of them had to be thrown overboard to pacify the waters. Sacrificing to rivers is ancient practice, the favorite sacrifice being virgins. Twain was but a virgin himself when he took to the river. These days, however, it's most likely that the river will snatch satellite antennas from the roofs of yuppie havens.

On the Illinois side of the river, a sorry bunch of people were packing everything they had in a peeling motorboat: mattresses, chairs, an oblong mirror that didn't fit anywhere, and boxes of clothes. My heart went out to them. The poor of West Quincy, unlike the well-off guardians of the tourist relics in Hannibal, were unprotected by levees. Most of them had no flood insurance, either. The question of flood insurance was an open wound. "It's expensive. We was in church this morning and the preacher told about Noah and said, 'He insured himself,' " an old black man said, while he helped load his neighbors' belongings. That morning, the congregation had prayed, sung "Amazing Grace," and got ready to leave their homes.

A father standing there with his fourteen-year-old son told me, "I brought him to see history. When I was a boy my father brought me to watch the flood in 1951." Someone standing nearby piped in, "My father brought me to watch in 1973." Some other people joined in and, one by one, they recalled all the major floods of their lifetimes. That was their history. In New Orleans, where I live, the conversation often turns to hurricanes. People remember each one and mark the past with its gales. In California, it was earthquakes.

In Europe, when I was growing up, folks remembered all their wars, big and small. At family gatherings, the oldest people would sing World War I songs until they fell asleep. Then it was the turn of World War II, until only the youngest were still awake, laughing at their elders, but knowing in their bones that their own dark hour wasn't far off.

History is an unrelenting chain of disasters in the memories of indi-

viduals. Sure, people remember happy occasions too, but they are usually ones that mark the conclusion of some great disaster. V-day. V-J
Day. If we have happy memories, they are usually private. What we
share with the world is an unbroken lament. But it isn't all sorrowful.
Catastrophes makes us feel insignificant: we are in awe of great forces
like raging rivers and quaking earth, events that show us just how puny
we are in the scheme of things. Such swift lessons in humility are joy-
ful occasions, actually, despite or, perhaps, because of the pain. Deep
down we are all doubtful of the illusion of control we pretend in our lives.
We suspect our own arrogance and feel guilty about it. When we stand
corrected by larger instances we experience pleasure. History is composed exclusively of the stories of our humbling. We watched the flood-
waters, secretly hoping to drown. Still, only the Quincy side had been
profoundly humbled. On the Hannibal side, after gazing at the river, the
folks went visiting Twain's house, Becky Thatcher's cottage, ogled Tom
Sawyer's still very white "fence," the most admired scam in American
history, and went to Mark Twain's Diner for lunch, where the onion rings
were as large as pilots' wheels, but composed of sheer grease. After
lunch, they went back to look at the river some more and argued about
the height, some of them opining that it had gone down an inch, others
that it hadn't.

I asked a young boy what he wanted to be when he grew up. "A me-
chanic," he said. I quoted Mark Twain to him: "When I was a boy, there
was but one permanent ambition among my comrades in our village. . . .
That was to be a steamboatman."

"Well," the boy confessed, "I been fishing and rowing on the river,
but when I grow up I wanna build engines."

Another boy, a serious-minded youngster with the face of an old
farmer already etched in his baby fat, pointed to the flooded silos: "Big
catfish in there. See where the current swirls? That's a cave, right under
there."

He had other things to say because he knew how to read the river,
but his father interrupted: "I was flooded out four years in a row. I sold
the farm last year. I work for the Army Corps now."

It was ironic, to say the least. "What did you grow?" I asked him.

"Soybeans and corn."

I wondered if he knew the long history that had led to his farming,
the vast engineering that had nearly turned the Mississippi into an in-
terstate highway, destroying sandbars, wetlands, fish, and wildlife.
Where his farm was, there had once been a floodplain that had been

the river's home. The straitjacket of levees and dams that had allowed him to farm was paid for with far more than his crops brought in. Surprisingly, he understood only too well. "I have never taken the river for granted," he said, "and I teached my son never to take it for granted. But man's gotta make a living."

It was an argument I would hear more of in the next few days. One of the better-spoken folk was a farmer from the Illinois side of the river, whose farm lay now under nine feet of water. "These are fertile plains. Asking us not to farm them is like putting a Thanksgiving feast before you and saying, 'Don't eat.' "

"Well, that's the problem," I said, too quickly. "People think of nature as a meal. It's there for us to eat."

"Yes," he replied, "but when you're hungry you eat."

There it was, in simple form, an argument that had been made since the Dust Bowl, leading to the federal government's Pick-Sloan Program to harness the Missouri in 1944. The rich soil of the Mississippi and its tributaries was too precious a resource to overlook for the sake of a larger picture. The Big Muddy is food. "A man that drunk Mississippi water could grow corn in his stomach if he wanted to," wrote Mark Twain. It was easy to see the flaws in the thinking of these river farmers and settlers, but it was not so easy to look into their faces and dismiss their pain. The people who'd come to gaze at the river, despite official warnings to stay away, were not driven by idle curiosity. The river was in their bones and in their dreams. They were soberly drawn to its rage. They knew that the river was mad at them.

In Quincy, people worked around the clock making sandbags. During a break, I asked a young shirtless man with a snake tattooed on his muscular arm what Mark Twain would have thought of their efforts. "He would've said: Let it rip! He woulda got a bottle of whiskey, settled on a hill, and watched the water come!" He spit toward the levee, crushed the cigarette butt under his foot, and got back to work. That was the heart of the matter. He knew, like everyone else, that their desperate industry was doomed to failure. He proceeded against the odds nonetheless. On Friday, the levee broke, and the water rushed in, covering fourteen thousand acres, including the entrance to the Bayview Bridge, the only passable bridge along a two-hundred-mile stretch of river from St. Louis to Burlington, Iowa. Mark Twain on his hill, with his bottle of whiskey, shook his head.

Medical authorities issued continual warnings against touching the water. The water had been contaminated by flooded sewage treatment plants and gas stations. There was a line of people getting shots at the hospital. There was talk here of the strike threatened by the workers at the treatment plants in St. Louis, a move that would threaten the city's water supply. The timing was opportunistic, even callous, but surprisingly, not many folks found this action objectionable. "People's got to eat," came the refrain, usable, it seemed, in all contingencies. On the other hand, people grinned when someone announced that the casino boats were still open, though one boat had to build its own bridge where the old one flooded. "The dice are rolling!" a man said triumphantly, as if at this sober time, the activity of losing money proved, somehow, the strength of the human spirit. Not all irony was lost, however. When I asked how the new contamination would affect the river, one of them said, quite sensibly: "It's already just garbage!"

In New Orleans it is said that "each glass of water from the Mississippi was drunk six times." And it's water that glows in the dark. Mark Twain's Mississippi has undergone the taming and toxic effects of civilization for over a century now. Spills, poisons, and floating garbage have choked its constrained flows. Twain reports that one of his friends had called the river "the great sewer." That was more than one hundred years ago. What he would have called it now is anyone's guess. It is a testimony to the strength of its being that the Mississippi is still alive after the numberless tons of chemical fertilizer, chemical compounds and who-knows-what poisons that were dumped in it. Here in New Orleans, mounds of radioactive gypsum wash right into the water courtesy of the "chemical corridor" or "cancer alley" between New Orleans and Baton Rouge. A friend of mine argued before the city council to stop the storing of gypsum along the river. The council members claimed that our filtration pumps remove all the chemicals from the water. It took a very long time to explain to the city fathers that radioactivity is not a chemical. The gypsum hasn't been moved. New Orleans keeps drinking Mississippi River water. Some of New Orleans, that is. Many of us drink bottled water. In the last mayoral election, the losing candidate said, "Uptown you drink Kentwood, downtown you get cancer." But how safe is Kentwood or all the other bottled water when the water table floats so high we bury our dead above ground? And gypsum is but one of the names of the river-killers that enter the stream courtesy of, among others, Hooker Chemicals, Dow Chemicals, B. F. Goodrich, E. I. Du Pont, Union Carbide, Texaco, Exxon, Uniroyal, Nalco Chemical, Freeport McMorran, Rubicon Chemicals—a string of well-lit, smoking cities that glow in the night like a party of devils along the Mississippi.

In fact, the Mississippi River between New Orleans and the Gulf of Mexico is engineered more carefully than any other part of the river for the purpose of keeping those industries in business. One would think that by the time the abused river gets to New Orleans, there would be little fight left in it. Walking toward the river on certain streets in New Orleans, you lift your eyes and see a huge commercial vessel looming over your head. The river, bound by the levee, is above street level. It is a strange feeling but it is nothing compared to standing on the huge lock at Old River in southern Louisiana, the spectacular Army Corps of Engineers project intended to contain Old Man River's passion for the younger, swifter Atchafalaya. So far the Mississippi hasn't yet jumped its traditional channel to merge with his beloved, but it's only a matter of time. But what's time to a river in love? Looking into the roaring waters of the Mississippi dropping twelve feet into the Atchafalaya (in quantities regulated by the Corps) I had the feeling that the Old Man would get his way. After traversing the better part of the continent, suffering the indignities of dams, levees, and poisons, the Mississippi has enough reserves to merge with the object of its passion. The course of the Atchafalaya to the Gulf is 145 miles, half the distance the Mississippi takes to get there. John McPhee, writing about the merger of the two rivers in *The Control of Nature*, said: "For the Mississippi to make such a change was completely natural, but in the interval since the last shift Europeans had settled beside the river, a nation had developed, and the nation could not afford nature."

In 1993, it seems, the nation cannot afford the consequences of its meddling with nature, either. The floods will have cost billions and billions of dollars that will mean nothing if we don't learn the essential lesson: let the river take its course.

Whenever I told someone in Hannibal that I was from New Orleans, they wanted to know what will happen when the big water gets to my house. I told them that I had heard an Army Corps general say that the dams and levees would probably take care of it. But that was, ironically, only part of the story. The Ohio River, which joins the Mississippi at Cairo, usually carries more water than the upper Mississippi, and contributes more of the combined flow. The Ohio is below normal levels, which means that the amount of water flowing past New Orleans is well within the river's capacity. In the end, it was the arrangement of the waters themselves that dictated the situation, the general's pride notwithstanding.

One of the black folks loading up his belongings on the boat told me that "won't nothing change until Mr. Twain comes back." On behalf of the writer, I tried not to smile. Twain, who believed in God as much as he believed in sandbagging "the great Mississippi, the magnificent Mississippi," would have been mightily amused to hear himself transformed into a sort of messiah. He would not have been amused by the state of the river in 1993. But then, he had already known the future: "When I was a boy, I looked into the river and I saw my reflection. And I said, 'Who's that?' My mother said, 'Samuel Langhorne Clemens.' In 1882 I returned to Hannibal, a celebrated writer and lecturer and steamboat pilot. And I looked into the river again. And I saw the reflection of an old man. And now, I look into the river and I see no reflection at all. We all come and we all go, but not the river, the mighty Mississippi. . . ."

As I flew over the shimmering water back to my city, which like Venice, Italy, is doomed and thus feels keenly its transitory beauty, I said a silent thank you to the old writer. He'd been preparing me since childhood for life on the Mississippi.

Democracy: What Keeps It Ticking?

Does American democracy still work in the age of corporatism, consumerism, TV-couchism, talk-show-offism, and a myriad others *isms* which have rushed to fill the vacuum left by the demise of Communism? How does the American community fare in the age of hyphenated people and well-developed micro-discontents?

Many people are now applying themselves to these questions, but, in a sense, these questions can no longer be answered in the abstract. On the right, the din of rhetoric runs from Newt Gingrich's science-fiction "revolution" to Rush Limbaugh's populist rabble-rousing. On the left, the necessity to defend gains in civil rights and environmental protection has precluded a clear expression of principles. The right has captured the government by being against it, while the left seems to defend the government that it was fighting only a decade ago. The strange redefinition of the political spectrum has rendered such directions as right and left mostly meaningless. As someone on my Greyhound bus commute said to me, while showering contempt on the whole lot of them: "It's all just words."

We have come a long way from the founding of America when Thomas Jefferson and George Washington could sit in the Apollo Room of the Raleigh Tavern in Williamsburg, Virginia, and use words to define American democracy as a nation based on words. The Mayflower Compact, the Declaration of Independence, and the Bill of Rights were the words that have kept American democracy functional. The founders were surely aware of the difference between demagoguery and vision and they had the good fortune to live in times that favored vision. In the age of talk shows, or "the epoch of endless blah-blah," as my Greyhound sage also put it, much of our language has been devalued. George Orwell's "newspeak," practiced so well in the once-Communist world, now holds sway over us as well. How we rescue community from the debris of isms is a universal question today.

The emergence of democracies in the former Communist world looks like a hopeless mass of confusion, but something exemplary lives in the primal goo. Forty years of Communism have indeed created a "new man," but this was not the idealized product that the fathers of Communism had been dreaming about. This creature was a passive cynic, distrustful of official pronouncements, but civically helpless. The only communal skills he possessed were an ability to barter, bargain, and dissimulate in order to survive. Paradoxically, the ideology of Communism decommunalized the citizens. Learning once more how to speak freely, congregate openly, and speak the truth amounts to nothing less than the reinvention of one's entire social being. How to do this while competing in the new marketplaces of ideas and products is unimaginably difficult. The people of former Communist countries have the job of re-creating community while affirming individuality and capitalism.

By comparison, our dilemmas seem less challenging. Two hundred years of American life, with its traditions of self-reliance, volunteerism, and individualism, have given us the resources to survive the current politics of crankiness and rhetorical ill will.

Alexis de Tocqueville, the Frenchman to whom we return so often when we reassess American democracy, admired the risk-taking, feverish optimism of Americans over the caution of Europeans. What we admire in the author of *Democracy in America* is his genuine surprise at the industrious civic life of average Americans. That sense of surprise is not diminished when the outside world looks at America now. Even those who deplore the successes of our popular culture over native expressions have to admit to American ingenuity and energy. The people of post-Communist countries are trying to learn in a hurry what makes us so productive. Western Europeans are attempting a United States of their own, modeled in part on us.

But the view from within is not quite the same. If one did nothing but watch television or listen to the speeches of politicians one might imagine this country as a cynical, exhausted, middle-aged nation that is spinning out of control. Yet nothing can be further from the truth. Getting off the couch into the neighborhood, and then onto the highway, and off onto the side roads, one finds a still-vigorous America. People one rarely sees on television are daily creating the miracles of functioning democracy.

The volunteer fire department is a familiar feature of small-town America. Social clubs, veterans organizations, church-based charities, and philanthropic associations have been a constant presence in American life. The end of the nineteenth century was a time of unprecedented energy, a time of enthusiastic waves of immigrants, new social movements, and utopian communities. It was also an epoch of rapid industrialization, brutal suppression of dissent, and the various tragic legacies of the Civil War. The civic organizations that emerged at this time were in direct response to the cries for help from Americans in need of material, spiritual, and philosophical nourishment. Walt Whitman, Henry David Thoreau, John Humphrey Noyes, Joseph Smith, the Shakers, the Chautauqua societies, the Arts and Crafts Movement were some of the answers.

The crises of our day call for different solutions. The disintegration of cities—great constructs themselves of the nineteenth century—demands urban heroes. And they are here. In one of New York's poorest neighborhoods, the Bedford-Stuyvesant Ambulance Corps is a grassroots organization that saves lives both literally and figuratively, by giving young people a sense of purpose. They are not "waiting for the government" to do something, according to Rocky Robinson, the director of the volunteer service. The same philosophy inspires the Hispanic activist Ernie Cortez, who speaks of taking "private pain into public action" and not allowing our "social capital" to unravel. In Englewood, near Chicago, a lending circle of African-American women are one another's collateral for small business loans. In Philadelphia, teenagers caught defacing property with graffiti enroll in an art program that transforms them into muralists.

Resistance to new immigration is one of the hottest demagogical tickets to political power today. Yet, one can point to Chinese immigrant Pauline Lo Alker, who runs Network Peripherals, a forty-million-dollar business. This is an extraordinary case, but success stories on a smaller scale are not hard to come by. Cities are being revitalized by neighborhoods of new immigrants.

Democracy faces new challenges in our time, but they would not have surprised the thinkers of the nineteenth century who were already familiar with many of the tensions and paradoxes between government, civil society, and capitalism. The limits and possibilities of freedom have to be weighed against opportunities for everyone. Grass-roots democracy emphasizes responsibility, yet corporate loyalties may overpower individual initiatives. Capitalism calls for less regulation, yet the environment needs to be protected. The resourcefulness of entrepreneurs and inventors comes right up sometimes against old patents and big business. Adding to this explosive mix, which was already familiar to our nineteenth-century predecessors, are the new facts of the mediated politics, the worlds of television, cyberspace, and market research.

In their way, each of the people mentioned before, leaders born of the immediate demands of their communities, serves to caution us against mistaking the vastness of the problems for their insolvability. They also refute the conventional clichés about minorities and immigrants. These people work to empower others, without waiting for government handouts or approval. Ernie Cortez's Iron Rule could serve as a motto for this new, yet traditional America: "Never do for someone what they can do for themselves."

America is an extraordinary web of civic, volunteer, and grass-roots organizations that tends to the life of her communities. The mainstream associations are supplemented by an inexhaustible number of emerging, new, even eccentric forms of community life. The question before politicians is how to support these efforts. The pitfalls shadow the opportunities. The age of cyberspace can either strengthen the civic fabric by bringing people together or it can tear it apart by commercializing it out of reach. The government can either insure the freedom of this new communications medium or it can hand it over to commercial interests. Too much regulation can stifle it, too little can choke it. This is only one example of the paradoxical role of government in a democracy.

A government that helps people help themselves is best for Americans. In this sense, the critics of the right understand the mood of the people when they berate the size and inefficiency of the government bureaucracy. But the critics on the left are equally accurate when they call for compassion and human values before cutting services and help to the poor.

When one travels the breadth and length of the United States, the TV-news-inspired picture of a cynical, tired country disappears. The questions of our time, with their attendant dilemmas, become personalized and immediate. The faces of citizens who do the real work of democracy appear on the real canvas instead.

Democracy on the Skin

I can still feel the bump at the side of my head where my stepfather whacked me when I once whispered, "Gheorghiu-Dej is a fat pig!" That smack echoed, in fact, an older smack delivered to me by a policeman's wife, an otherwise kind woman, who was my baby-sitter. In that case, I had been lying in the sun on her front steps and when I got too hot, I said: "Goddamn the sun!" She slapped me so swiftly I thought it was lightning. "Don't ever say that about the sun!" she thundered. Those two smacks were early instances of political education. Gheorghiu-Dej, the aforementioned fat pig, was Romania's Communist dictator in the fifties. The sun, which I apologize even now for insulting, was the Romanians' pre-Christian God. Gheorghiu-Dej ruled the country a lot like the sun.

When I left Romania in the midsixties, I met my first democracy in Naples, Italy, where they were selling Bibles and porn magazines on the street. This was so amazing an expression of liberty to me that I stood amazed before the newsstand and delivered at the top of my lungs a paean of praise to freedom and democracy. I was, however, unbeknownst to me, praising capitalism. Most amazingly, I wasn't arrested for it, though I did get looks. That part of it was democracy.

A couple of years later in Detroit, Michigan, where I came to live, the same kind of speech *could* get you arrested, especially during the 1967 riots when National Guard tanks rumbled right past my house near Woodward Avenue. In 1968, during a demonstration against the war in Vietnam, I got smacked on the head by a cop's nightstick. That particular smack confused my notions of freedom and democracy somewhat, making me wonder whether they were the same thing. That became the burning question both East and West, in Prague and in Chicago. Democracy became decoupled from capitalism at that time because young people disdained the gross consumerism of their elders. But as the decades rolled by and we settled snugly into the forgiving arms of the military-industrial-entertainment complex, questions of democracy and freedom changed to the answer, which was: capitalism *über Alles.*

In 1989 and thereabouts, the Commies gave up the ghost of tyranny and you could barely hear the collapsing of walls from the strains of that triumphant tune. I went back to Romania to find that stepfather and the policeman's wife who smacked me, hoping to smack them back. I didn't find them, but even if I had they were probably horribly old and starving to death because the new capitalism that came along with democracy made their pensions worthless. Their children had, doubtless, joined one of the new antidemocratic, nationalist parties that infest the old Red Empire now. Among the targets of their wrath are Jews, émigrés, and Americans. That's me—bingo! The chances for getting smacked were excellent. Happily, I was there with NPR and ABC News who made sure that democracy, along with my hide, were not to be trifled with.

What have I learned about democracy in a lifetime of being smacked from the left and the right? Only one thing really: it's a good thing, but it ought not to be mixed with capitalism as if they were one thing. Democracy is an equal-opportunity smacker. Capitalism smacks everybody.

Whose **Woods** Are **These**?

Whose woods these are I think I know.
His house is in the village though;
He will not see me stopping here
To watch his woods fill up with snow.

—ROBERT FROST, *"Stopping by Woods on a Snowy Evening"*

After having been in America for nearly thirty years I am only an immigrant because people want me to talk about it. Would you ask Henry Kissinger to talk on the subject of "American Foreign Policy: An Immigrant's Experience"? Still, I am more of an immigrant than Henry only because or precisely because I *have* been talking about it lately. Paradoxically, it was a recent return to Romania, my native country, that has caused me to reevaluate my American experience. Until that time I considered myself a model American: drank Jim Beam, wore Converse high tops, quit smoking on tax day. Of course, I may have been *too* perfect.

I went back to Romania in December 1989 to report on the so-called revolution over there but, in truth, I went back in order to smell things.

I went there to recover my childhood. I wanted to take deep breaths in the old squares of my hometown. I went around sniffing the stones of the medieval tower under the Liars' Bridge where I used to lie still like a lizard in the summer. I put my cheek against the tall door of our old house, built in 1456, with its rusty smell of iron. I sniffed past people's windows to see what they were cooking. There were aromas of *paprikash* and strudel, and the eternal cabbage.

(When all masonry has crumbled, all human habitation gone, there will still be a faint smell of cabbage wafting over Eastern Europe the way it still wafts out of the tenements of the Lower East Side in New York. It's curious: the early European immigrants who inhabited those New York tenements are mostly gone but the smell of cabbage still wafts, mixed with the frying pork and jalapeños of the newer Hispanic arrivals. Someone ought to do a history of immigration based on stinks, scents, smells, and aromas. At what point do the pungent cuisines of one's native land vanish in the deodorized commuter traffic of America?

I made my way into the past through my nose, madeleinizing everything. My childhood, which had been kept locked and preserved in the crumbling city of Hermanstadt, in the centrum, was still there, untouched. It had outlasted my immigration, it was one thousand years old.

Considering then that childhood lasts for one thousand years, the last thirty years of adulthood in America do not seem like such a big deal. Of course, sniffing was not why NPR had paid my way back to Romania so I had to file some "real" stories as well. These were about adults and adult issues, which were nowhere near as interesting as my childhood. My old friends, now adults, had metamorphosed in the past twenty-five years into—mostly—fat survivors of a miserable and baroque system where material things were the supreme spiritual value. For them, America was the heavenly Wal-Mart. That's what God was during Communism because God was every-thing and everything can be found at Wal-Mart. Thank God, they didn't know about the Mall of America or they'd be here right now, a barefoot procession that would clog your splendid highway system. Forty years of so-called Communism have done no more than polish to perfection my grandmother's maxim, "In America dogs walk around with pretzels on their tails." Loose translation: In America the sidewalks are paved with gold.

I had fantasized coming back to my country a celebrated author, envied by all the people who made my life hell in high school. But now I wished, more than anything, that I'd come back a Wal-Mart. If only I were a Wal-Mart, I could have spread my beauteous aisles to the awestruck of Hermanstadt and fed them senseless with all the bounty of America.

> *If I were a Wal-Mart*
> *And you were my past*
> *Would you make me back a child*
> *Would you make it last?*

That's what I sang. The fact is that I would trade adulthood for childhood in a minute, and mine wasn't all that great.

When I came back to America I reeled about for a few days in shock. Everything was so new, so carelessly abundant, so thoughtlessly shiny, so easily taken for granted. The little corner store with its wilted lettuce and the spotted apples was a hundred times more substantial than the biggest, bare-shelf store in Romania.

I remembered that my mother, ever a practical woman, started investing in furniture when she came to America. Not any furniture. Sears furniture. Furniture that she kept the plastic on for fifteen years before she had to conclude, sadly, that Sears furniture wasn't such a great investment. In Romania she would have been the richest woman on the block.

Which brings us to at least one paradox of immigration. Most people come here because they are sick of being poor. They want to eat and they want to show something for their industry. But soon enough it becomes evident to them that it isn't enough. They have eaten and they are full, but they have eaten alone and there was no one to make toasts and sing songs. They have new furniture with plastic on it, but the neighbors aren't coming over to *ooh* and *aah*. If neighbors, American neighbors or less recent immigrants, do come over, they smile condescendingly at the poor taste and the pathetic greed. And so, the greenhorns find themselves poor once more: this time they are lacking something more elusive than salami and furniture. They are bereft of a social and cultural milieu. Immigration is cruel to new immigrants: they are mostly invisible to Americans—except as objects of dismay and subjects of political demagoguery—and their fellow immigrants, with few exceptions, are in a hurry to forget their cultures and get on with the business of melting.

My mother, who was middle class by Romanian standards, found herself immensely impoverished after her first flush of material well-being. It wasn't just the disappearance of her milieu—that was obvious—but the feeling that she had, somehow, been had. The American supermarket tomatoes didn't taste at all like the rare genuine item back at home. American chicken was tasteless. Mass-produced furniture was built to fall apart. Her car, the crowning glory of her achievements in the eyes of folks back at home—was only three years old and was already beginning to wheeze and groan. It began to dawn on my mother that she had perhaps made a bad deal: she had traded in her friends and relatives for fake chicken, ersatz tomatoes, and phony furniture.

Leaving behind your kin, your friends, your language, your smells, your childhood is traumatic. It is a kind of death. You're dead for the home folk and they are dead to you. When you first arrive on these shores you are in mourning. The only consolation are these products, which had been imbued with religious significance back at home. But when these things turn out not to be the real things, you begin to experience a second death, brought about by betrayal. You begin to suspect that the religious significance you had attached to them was only possible back home where these things did not exist. Here, where they are plentiful, they have no significance whatsoever. They are inanimate fetishes, somebody else's fetishes, no help to you at all. When this realization dawned on my mother, she began to rage against her new country. She deplored its rudeness, its insensitivity, its outright meanness, its indifference, the chase after the almighty buck, the social isolation of most Americans, their inability to partake in warm, genuine fellowship and, above all, their deplorable lack of awe before what they had made.

This was the second stage of grief for her old self. The first, leaving her country, was sharp and immediate, almost tonic in its violence. The second was more prolonged, more damaging, because no hope was attached to it. Certainly, not the hope of return.

And here, thinking of return, she began to reflect that perhaps there had been more to this deal than she'd first thought. She had left behind a lot that was good, it was true, but she had also left behind a vast range of daily humiliations. If she was ordered to move out of town she had to comply. If a Party member took a dislike to her she had to go to extraordinary lengths to placate him because she was considered petit bourgeois and could have easily lost her small photo shop. She lived in fear of being denounced for something she had said. And worst of all, she was a Jew, which meant that she was structurally incapable of obtaining any justice in her native land. She had lived by the grace of an immensely complicated web of human relations, kept in place by a thousand small concessions, betrayals, indignities, bribes, little and big lies. In addition to the strictures of her petit bourgeois status she was bound to the generalized lie of the Communist state by a million small lies of survival.

She had lived at home inside a cautious silence which was the second nature of everyone she knew. Publicly, no one spoke the truth. The newspapers lied about everything, except the sports scores. (And even those were subject to Party approval.) When people said something out loud it wasn't for the person they were speaking to, it was for "the ear in the wall." At home, speaking to one's intimates, one whispered, but even this whisper was mostly a lie because "the ear in the wall" was both in the inside and the outside wall. And when one spoke privately to one's own self, that was still a lie because "the ear in the wall" had become one's very own ear.

So, as much as my mother loved the tiny living room of our precious mini-apartment on the Workers's Victory Boulevard, it was not hers. It belonged to the state, like everything else, including her words.

At this point in her reminiscence, the ersatz tomato and the faux chicken did not appear all that important. An imponderable had made its appearance, a bracing, heady feeling of liberty. If she took that ersatz tomato and flung it at the head of the agriculture secretary of the United States, she would be making a statement about the disastrous effects of pesticides and mechanized farming. Flinging that faux chicken at Louise Mandrell would be equally dramatic and perhaps even mediaworthy. What's more, she didn't have to eat those things, because she could buy organic tomatoes and free-range chicken. Of course, it would cost more, but that was one of the paradoxes of America: to eat as well as people in a third-world country eat *when* they eat, it costs more.

My mother was beginning to learn two things: one, that she had gotten a good deal after all because in addition to food and furniture they had thrown in freedom, and two, America is a place of paradoxes: one proceeds from paradox to paradox like a chicken from the pot into the fire.

And that's where I come in. My experience was not at all like that of my mother. I came here for freedom, not for food. I came here in the midsixties. Young people East and West at that time had a lot more in common with each other than with the older generations. The triple-chinned hogs of the *nomenklatura* who stared down from the walls of Bucharest were equal in our minds to the Dow Chemical pigs who gave us napalm and Vietnam. By the time I left Romania in 1966, the Iron

Curtain was gone: a Hair Curtain fell between generations. Prague 1968 and Chicago 1968 were on the same axis: the end of the old world had begun.

Our anthems were the songs of Dylan, the Beatles, the Rolling Stones, all of whom were roundly despised by my mother because she was sure that such tastes would lead to our being thrown out of America. And she wasn't all that wrong: her old don't-rock-the-boat instinct was an uncannily fine instrument. At that time, being antiestablishment in America was as threatening as being antiestablishment in Romania. There was a difference, of course, the massive, albeit expensive, difference of the constitutional right to freedom of speech and assembly. But for a moment or two there—and for several long, scary moments since—those constitutional rights were in real danger. And if Americans were threatened, you can imagine that many niceties of those laws simply didn't apply to refugees.

Nonetheless, I was drunk with freedom and I wasn't about to dilute my euphoria with the age-old wariness of Eastern Europeans. I didn't want to eat anything. My mother's main pleasure and strategy in those days was to overstuff me whenever I came to visit. She believed that food would anchor me and keep me safe. Food keeps you from going out at night, it makes you sleepy, makes you think twice about hitchhiking, makes you, generally, less radical. The very things that alienated my mother—the speed, confusion, social unrest, absence of ceremony—exhilarated me. I had arrived here at an ecstatic moment in history and I was determined to make the most of it. And when, thanks to the marketing know-how of the CIA, I got to try LSD for the first time, I became convinced that freedom was infinitely vaster than was generally acknowledged. It was not just a right, it was an atmosphere. It was the air one needed to breathe. And one had to stay skinny.

Nowadays, that glimpse, that vision, has dimmed considerably. Proportional to the flesh, I'd say. Those who may have inadvertently opened that cosmic window have been endeavoring to close it ever since. And my mother's refrigerator, a conservative god, has lumbered to the center of life, filled to the rafters with little plastic baggies full of orderly calculations.

In 1966, my generation welcomed me into its alienated and skinny arms with a generosity born of outsiderness. All young people at that time had become outsiders to America's mainstream. Those who went to Vietnam were way outside even though, ostensibly, they served the inside. The others were in voluntary exile from the suburbs all immigrants hoped to one day live in. But what mattered is that we were all on the move. I happened to be a literal exile in a world of, mostly, metaphorical exiles. It was a match made in heaven. America was nineteen years old and so was I. I lived in a country of exiles, a place that had its own pantheon of elders, exiled geniuses like Einstein and Nabokov, and whole nomad youth armies. Exile was a place in the midsixties, an international idea-state, the only anarchist state in working order. It's not the kind of thing that comes around all that often in American immigrant history. It is not even the thing most immigrants dream about when they dream of America.

I've already mentioned the pretzels.

There have been many immigrant visions of America in the four hundred years since Europeans first came here, most of them a variation of *Ubi pretzel ibi patria*, but the true, ineffable one was not a pretzel but a pear, Charles Fourier's pear to be exact. For Fourier, the pear was the perfect fruit. It was to be eaten in paradise by lovers. This vision of a utopian New World was entirely about freedom. The freedoms granted by the Bill of Rights were only the steps leading to this new state of being.

The prophetic tradition that maintains that America is chosen among nations to bring about the end of history is not just an extension of European Communist ideas. It is also an ingrained American belief, one that, it can be argued, has kept America strong, vigorous, and young. Walt Whitman's America was done with the niceties of Europe because it was bigger, ruder, and it had a greater destiny. This America was also a country of immigrants who gave it their raw muscle and imagination. Diversity and industry were its mainstays. Even Allen Ginsberg, a bitter prophet at the end of the 1950s, could say, "America, I put my queer shoulder to the wheel." Despite the irony, Ginsberg, the son of a Russian Jewish immigrant, really believes that his queer shoulder is needed, that America needs not just its bankers but also its queers.

But this sustaining vision of America is, paradoxically again, marginal. It is often confused with another, similar-sounding creed, which is in all the textbooks and is invoked by politicians on the Fourth of July. This faux creed of an immigrant-built, patriotic nation-state is the official ideology which, like the party line in Romania, is meant to drive underground the true and dangerous vision. What's more, the rhetoric of this Americanism is written so that no one has to really believe it. In reality, few people do. What most Americans think that they *should* believe about America is not at all what they *really* believe about it and, if pressed, they will admit that only freaks believe such idealistic blather. Or, at the very least, they will admit to no contradiction between their love of freedom and their hatred of outsiders.

The history of the public opinion of immigration shows mainly resistance to it. There is nothing new about current anti-immigration sentiments. Most immigration after the mid-eighteenth century would have never happened if the majorities had had a say in it. They didn't because immigration was driven by a demand for labor. The farther away we got from the revolutionary ideas of the eighteenth century, the more it appeared that compassion for the wretched and persecuted of the earth was dictated by the interests of capitalists.

Not that this was necessarily bad. Heartless capitalism in its ever-growing demand for cheap labor saved millions of people from the no-exit countries of the world. It was a deal that ended up yielding unexpected and imponderable benefits: energy, imagination, the remaking of cities, new culture. Restless capital, restless people, ever-expanding boundaries—the freedom to move, pick up, start again, and shed the accursed identities of static native lands. . . . The deal turned out to have the hidden benefit of liberty. The liberty my mother discovered in America *was* here: it was a by-product of the anarchic flow of capital, the vastness of the American space, *and* a struggle in the name of the original, utopian vision. Of course, capitalism annexed the resulting moral capital and put on an idealistic face it never started out with, and which it quickly sheds whenever production is interrupted. Nonetheless, it is this capitalism with a human face that brought most of us here. And it is that human face, that mask of utopian kindness, that has found its way into textbooks and is sold to every child with a picture of Miss Liberty—that French immigrant—with the Emma Lazarus poem somewhat blurred underneath.

But this capitalism with a human face is not the same as the original vision of America. The original American dream is religious, socialist, and anticapitalist. It was this utopianism, liberty in its pure, unalloyed state that I experienced in nondenominational, ahistorical, uneconomical, transcendent flashes in the midsixties. It's not simple, dialectical Manicheism we are talking about here. It's the mystery itself.

A few years ago, hard-line anti-Communists told us that America was a haven for the politically oppressed. Today, the winners, without bothering to check if anything has truly changed, are telling us to stem immigration for our *economic* good. In other words, this is one of those times when capitalism with a human face can afford to take off its face and breathe. It isn't easy wearing your idealistic mask in public—for years. Also, capital isn't circulating so well in this middle-age of production.

If somebody had asked my mother in the midsixties if she was a political refugee, she would have answered, "Of course," but privately she would have scoffed at the idea. She was an economic refugee, a warrior in quest of Wal-Mart. In Romania she had been trained at battling in lines for every necessity. In America, at last, her skills would come in handy. Alas. But if somebody had asked me, I would have said, "I'm a planetary refugee, a professional refugee, a permanent exile." Not on my citizenship application form, of course. That might have been a bit dramatic, but in truth I never felt like a refugee, either political or economic. What I felt was that it was incumbent upon me to manufacture difference, to make myself as distinct and unassimilable as possible. To increase my foreignness, if you will. That was my contribution to America. Not the desire to melt, but the desire to embody an instructive difference.

Melting pot, boiling point. Boiling pot, melting point. Boiling. Melting. Pot. J. Hector St. John de Crèvecoeur first put the matter this way in 1769: "Here individuals of all nations are melted into a new race of men, whose labors and posterity will one day cause great changes in the world."

I have no doubt that this has come to pass. Crèvecoeur goes on to say: "What then is the American, the new man? He is either a European, or the descendant of a European, hence that strange mixture of blood, which you will find in no other country."

An American is a European man. I won't charge old Crack-Heart with retrospective sexism, but he does seem to have left out a couple of races. Native Americans and African Americans never melted into this new American man. And that makes the metaphor suspect.

Who is tending this pot? Who is stoking the flames? What's in this pot, really? Is it possible that the new American man, having successfully melted, now stands outside the pot, rocking it, while inside it, stubbornly refusing to melt, are all of America's others: Native Americans, African Americans, religious freaks, sexual freaks, extreme libertarians? Which is to say, all the original inhabitants plus the original devotees of the vision of utopian America. A curious situation this: the elements inside the pot that most refuse to melt are the *oldest* ones. What's going on here?

This all-purpose pot, is it not a metaphor for containment?

And, is it really a pot? Isn't it more of a cauldron?

And is a witch rocking it?

And if one were to rephrase St. John the Crack-Heart's question, "What then is the American, this new man?," I would have to say, paradoxically, of course, "A new arrival who hasn't yet arrived, but has been here all along, someone whose ambition is not to melt but to differ."

To the question "Whose woods are these?," which Robert Frost never asked because he thought that he already knew the answer—"Whose woods these are I think I know,"—my mother would have said, without hesitation, "Everybody else's." My mother, like most immigrants, knew only too well that these were somebody else's woods. She only hoped that one day she might have a piece of them. My answer to that question would have been, and I think still is, "Nobody's." These are nobody's woods and that's how they must be kept: open for everybody, owned by nobody. This is, in part at least, how Native Americans thought of them. It was a mistake, of course. Nobody's woods belong to the first marauding party who claims them. A better answer might be: "These woods belong to mystery; this is the forest of paradoxes, *una selva oscura*; we belong to them not they to us."

The Rosa Luxemburg Conference

O n the coldest day of the century in Chicago the remnants of the radical left braved the ice to gather at the Blue Rider Theater to take stock of socialism. It was so cold that a Russian man in the lobby of my hotel muttered: "We got rid of Communism, but Siberia's everywhere." It was a fitting remark, given the times and the elements.

Providing the spark for the meeting was Donna Blue Lachman, the playwright-performer of *The Language of Birds: Rosa Luxemburg and Me.* Rosa Luxemburg was a fiery revolutionary who led the German communists in the early days of the century. She was a passionate woman whose personal life and revolutionary politics meshed. She disagreed with Lenin's authoritarian methods and would have greatly influenced the course of socialism if she had lived. She was murdered by the fascists in 1919, along with fellow radical Karl Liebknecht. Donna Blue gave Rosa a renewed lease on life with her play, and now the participants at "Rosa Luxemburg: A Conference Where Artists and Revolutionaries Meet" were trying to do the same for socialism.

After the collapse of authoritarian Communism, the relentless attacks of the right, co-optation by bourgeois parties, the discrediting of its language—could socialism still mean something? I wasn't too sure. What I was sure of is that I liked the people in the room, especially the older ones, people with lively eyes, still fiercely interested in improving the world despite the battering and bruising of age, weather, and reality. Some of them even smoked cigarettes, an action so rare these days it qualified instantly for radical subversion.

I shared the stage with Leon Despres, a former Chicago socialist alderman, whose speeches had been notorious during Richard Daley Sr.'s authoritarian administration. Former Alderman Despres was of the deeply held opinion that Rosa Luxemburg and socialism will never die. I wasn't too sure about that, either, but then, once again, what can one do but feel affection for the idealists of the world, an endangered species? There were artists, anarchists, socialists, peaceniks, and actors in the room, defying Siberian weather, all of them smoky, luminous, betrayed, rare, and terribly alive.

Am **Myth**: Whazzit, Whozzit, Whozinonit?

Considering myth one has to stand before the word for a moment: there is capital *M* Myth, which is the kind of story that never changes, was, is, and will be; a story written by no one but told by everyone; a story that exists independently of its tellers; a story that cannot be changed by temporal circumstances; the elements of it may be updated, the language of it may be hipped, but the story stays the same.

Creation stories are myths of this type. "In the beginning was the Word," or "In the Beginning was Spider Woman," are stories that cannot be changed because they describe the activities of divine beings in the *illo tempore*, before history began. The actions of the gods at that time before time were completely significant and irreversibly generative. A gesture once made set worlds in motion. The description of that activity, carried into history by storytellers, had the function of abolishing time and putting its listeners or reenacters in a sacred time, outside history, in the *illo tempore* of the original divine activity.

The founding myths of nations belong to this category. The founding myth of Romania is Mioritza, the story of a love affair between a boy and a sheep. Most nations were founded, incidentally, by bestiality, incest, or some kind of taboo mix of humans and animals. Romans arrived in history on a stream of wolf's milk. We Romanians have sheep fucking at the founding of our nationhood.

In the Americas, the world before the white man was woven by a spider. But modern America, the white man's America, was born in history not in prehistory, so we have no gods. The God on the dollar bill is an eyeball, the eye of a camera, watching everything with the relative objectivity of science for which everything is equally significant. There is no *illo tempore* where the founding gestures continue unchanged. In fact, change is the only unchanging law.

"What does not change / is the will to change," said Charles Olson, a very big man and poet of oceanic verse, who sought to create an epic poem, "Maximus," that would contain both the founding mythology of America and its subsequent history.

Olson took the little town of Gloucester and proceeded to verbalize and dramatize its beginning with the geology of its rocks and the stories the Atlantic Ocean bequeathed to her fishermen. In employing the ocean, Olson borrowed shamelessly from the Greeks and the Phoenicians, seafaring people whose stories he found still agitating the foam. That was a bit of American disingenuity and brilliance: the poetic ocean is naturally made from all the stories told about it and almost all stories spring from the ocean. Dipping into it for myth is like shooting fish in a barrel, to mix a couple of containers. But in appropriating the myths for American use, Olson did that most American of activities: collage.

American myth is collage, as is just about everything else in America, except geography. Collage is the medium, par excellence, of our cultural story. We are a collage of cultures. Our storytelling is produced today by television, a collage medium. Our language is the language of images, which are collageable items. Myth-dipped Europeans sick of history set up America as a collage of their utopian yearnings. Here was paradise, streets paved with gold, dogs with pretzels on their tails—my grandmother's version—fertile soil, unlimited horizons, rivers of ale, mountains of salt. America, for immigrants, was posthistory, which is the same as prehistory. In European myths, everything happened at the beginning. In America, everything was going to happen in the end, in the future. Paradise and utopia met here and paved over the prehistory of the original inhabitants.

Every myth is the story of a quest: the hero overcomes the horrendous obstacles of temporality (or history) in order to find eternity (or utopia). For the Europeans, there was no Original Sin in America. All that stayed behind in Europe. America was Utopia, the end of the Quest, possible because the old had been left behind. This particular belief gave birth to another kind of myth. This is the sort of story that exists in a cluster of similar stories that form a "mythology" or a "mythography." Its salient feature is that it has been manufactured by a myth-making industry, Broadway, Hollywood, or Madison Avenue. The raw material of it was the yearning of immigrants faced with the challenges of American space.

The most enduring—relatively speaking—myths of this provenance are: in America you can start again; you can change your name and your face and be reborn; hard work (or luck), not history, is what matters; in America everything is possible; the reward of puritanism is hedonism; paradise is here and now—as the Oneida Community and the Living Theatre told us—we are mechanically gifted and will find a technological solution to everything.

We have a constitutional right to "the pursuit of happiness," which has now become "the relentless pursuit of happiness." In the beginning was the automated kitchen and the computer. Everything about America has to do with beginnings. We have no eschatology, no science of the end. In the afterlife, we begin again, just as if we were moving from New York to California. Our White Goddess is the refrigerator: she stands white and tall in the kitchen, drawing all, feared by all, giver of sustenance and source of fearful calories.

Some of the heroes of these American myths, or mechanomythography, are: the loner who conquers evil through grit and charm, the cowboy with a heart of gold, the whore with the rapier wit, the maladjusted emigrant who renews himself (me), the "destroyer of worlds"—Oppenheimer or Teller—and the Giver of Meaning, Vanna White.

Edward Teller and Vanna White, to take only two of these mechano-archetypes, represent two permanent features of the American soul: the male part that desires bigger and bigger explosions indifferently of cost, and the nurturing female who proves time after time that there is meaning in a meaningless universe, that there really are words, phrases, and things, in the lacunae between disconnected letters. The American quest, as exemplified by these two archetypes, is for a bright afterlife where meaning is guaranteed. Of course, we first have to surrender doubt and then die. This myth would not function if we refused to blow up or, at least, entertained some suspicion that behind the jumble of letters lies a Finnish word or, horror of horrors, a Dada word.

Edward Teller and Vanna White have no equivalents in ancient myth. She is a blond native born of the California imaging fields, and is a collage of many myths. She is a little bit like Isis who searched for the fourteen pieces of the body of Osiris and gathered them back together. This she does, not with a man, but with language every night on television. She is a little bit like Arachne, the girl famous in Greece for her skill at weaving. But there is no Athena to become jealous of her because Vanna has a good contract that protects her from just such contingencies.

Edward Teller is a collage, too. A Hungarian Jew who suffered the loss of a leg in prewar Germany, he developed the hydrogen bomb and was the father of the Star Wars program. In Europe his physical and mythical MO would have reminded everyone of the Wandering Jew, Mephistopheles, and Dr. Faustus. A bum leg is always the Devil's mark. But in America, Dr. Teller became an American myth: the god of technological preeminence based on the joy of apocalyptic fire.

Note the names: Vanna White, white, white, whiter than Snow White, who has whited out ambiguity, whitened the darkness of meaninglessness and chaos. And Teller, the teller of the story that begins in the darkness of medieval Europe and ends in the paradise of utopian America. The teller of the End and the White of the afterlife are myths of technology, American myths.

If one understands now the distinction between immutable myth and mutable mythmaking by American myth machines, I would like to introduce a third category of myth: artist-generated paradoxes whose function is to sabotage technomyths.

Ezra Pound said to Americans in American: "Make it new!" And that has been the imperative for all those who would generate an idea, a story, or an object. That was the mythical modern imperative. The paradox is that you cannot create a new myth of the *illo tempore* variety I mentioned earlier. You can only collage bits of existing myth in order to fabricate an operating story. And that's the story of the modern, from Cubism and Joyce's *Ulysses,* to Teller and Vanna.

One can argue that Vanna is postmodern but postmodernism, to me, is only a stylistic turn of the modern: the collaging imperative is the same, with the added adagio: "Get it used!" In other words, "Make it new" has suffered the necessary corrective, "Get it used," making it not just accurate but chic to use used materials. And the more used—the more ancient—the better. "Use-value" is the postmodern recognition that we needn't fool anyone: that the machinery of the illusion is chic and valuable, equally as "real" as the myth, object, or story.

Artist-generated collages become generalized cultural myths when they get big distribution. After that, they become automatic, generic received ideas with varying half-lives that float in the national psyche until they burn out. The machinery of illusion is a giant maw that needs artists' creations at an increasing rate. The mythical contest being currently played out is between the speed of the artist and the speed of the machine that would employ his or her stories. We have to make faster and faster to keep ahead of the dragon chasing us. Because once he catches us that's the end of any light at the end of the tunnel. *The machine prolongs the tunnel—into infinity.* And you can't turn around to run away either, because at the beginning of the tunnel is Mr. Teller, with the H-bomb in his hand, and at the end is Vanna, turning the letters.

In America, immutable myth, mechanomyth, and artist myth have to deal with one element which may or may not be purely American: space. Charles Olson begins his discussion of Melville with this assertion: "Space is the central fact of man in North America." We have done our best to abolish space technologically, and to banish the very ideas of the "outside." Yet, American space is what all our stories are about: the East-West journey, the vastness of the prairie, the marshes, the flood plains, the journey of the Mississippi.

Space is the one immutable—no matter how much we have tried to move it outside of our perception—character of our myth, mythography, and artistry.

A **Report** on the State of **Revolution**(s) for **Rosa** Luxemburg

Twenty years ago I wrote a poem called "Sunday Sermon":

> *All sound is religion.*
> *Language is merely a choirboy in this religion.*
> *Sometimes a bishop wind rattles the windows.*
> *Still, I must speak the most intelligent language available*
> *while I have this typewriter knowing full well that tomorrow*
> *I might be able to welcome a color Xerox machine into my*
> *   studio*
> *and with it there will be a revolution in my life.*
> *And this revolution will wipe out the need for words.*

I will say nothing for a few years to prepare for a new
revolution. Revolution. The word is like a revolver on a
sunlit window sill. It is one of the few words that sets
my heart on fire. Girl also sets my heart on fire.
Girl & revolution. Revolution & girl.
I am twelve years old and I intend to stay that way.

Now, that was 1974, and there were two revolutions—that I could
see—going on: a sexual revolution and a technological revolution. As
a matter of faith—and fun—I threw my lot in with the sexual revolution and felt quite hostile toward the technological revolution. Personally, I believed that enough things had already been produced and that
we could reuse them for five hundred years for every purpose, including collage, which is thing-intensive. The romance of information never
held any fascination for me because it was just one more river of things
with extensive penal obligations. Both palpable things and information
are time thieves.

The sex revolution, as I saw it, was a time maker: it expanded the
boundaries of time to infinity. Sex did that without things—without
clothes, actually—though a few objects may have been required for
fetish purposes. And that's why, incidentally, the sex revolution had its
headquarters in California. Looking at the four-dimensional map of that
revolution we could see the bright pink centers in the tropics with the
cold-climate fetish zones swimming underneath wrapped in layers of severe rhetoric. Penetration of these layers would be accomplished by the
Living Theatre, which at the time of this description would have grown
to the approximate size of the Judeo-Masonic conspiracy.

Let me explain: in 1969 in Detroit, Michigan, a cold-zone similar to
Chicago, Alice and I put up several members of the Living Theatre
cast—in town performing *Paradise Now*—at our quasi-communal pad
on John Lodge, and in the morning all five of them came to breakfast
NAKED! The nice midwestern hippies-in-the-making inhabiting our
household were shocked—I was—but we all pretended that it was very
normal to have breakfast naked. So we pretended that nothing was unusual even as we burnt the toast because we weren't watching it. Of
course, after that, we came to breakfast naked whenever we were visiting anybody, and this naked thing spread. I mean, visiting anybody our
age, because it wasn't either easy or somehow rewarding being naked
at one's parents' house.

At the successful conclusion of this revolution we had a Mao-like plan to have cities of approximately the same size exchange populations: Chicago, for instance, would have exchanged with Los Angeles. The long disco-trains—turbo-trains—of the sex revolution would have reenacted for the masses the migratory flights of the artistic petite bourgeoisie that was, at the time, restlessly flying the skies of United in search of warmer selves. The technology needed for these trains was transitory since we were also working on telepathic teleportation.

In the fourth dimension, the Garden of Eden was located in the backyard where Mr. and Mrs. Blake sat, surrounded by the smog of fin-de-nineteenth-century London, under a puny tree struggling through cement, from whose branches hung a reel of film, some primitive sexual apparatus, and passion fruit dribbling juice. I'm not sure, but the passion fruit may have doubled as primitive sexual apparatus. The film, incidentally, was produced akhashakikally from the memories of humanity's tiny instances of pleasure, all of which could be put on a single reel.

Both revolutions, the sexy and the techy, demanded sacrifices. The sexual revolution required that one remain in a twelve-year-old's state of perpetual excitement. It also demanded that one dispense with the paraphernalia of personal and class psychology, as well as economic determinism and idealized body shapes. I was quite willing to do that I am Romanian and our nation was born of the union of a sheep with a boy who was assassinated for his property, leaving the sheep to wander disconsolately through the deserts of inchoate history, giving an esthetically pleasing, cosmogonic description of the cancerous growth of the universe. Under those circumstances, congress with another human was mythically bound to dispense with time, thought, space, and matter.

The technological revolution, on the other hand, demanded of me that I give up words and remain underground until some as-yet-unnamed revolution gave me back my expression. Note too that the tech revolution I was envisioning—I'm now glossing the opening poem, which you may have forgotten—was not about the computer and its power to process a seemingly infinite number of words, but about copying, which would permit only the infinite reproduction of what was already there. The threat was distribution, not production. In order to protest excessive distribution I was quite prepared to give up production.

The means of reproduction available to us in those days, by means of which we intended to seize the means of reproduction that would render us mute, was the mimeograph machine. Our ink-stained hands like the ink-stained hands of all the revolutionaries before us produced many poetic manifestos. I now ask you to pause for the moment in the darkness of the revolutionary print shop. That smell of ink and lead contains the romance of revolution. It's all in there. Rosa Luxemburg standing anxiously over the printer setting type for her lead article in *Sprawa Robotnicza*. Lenin watching the first issue of *Pravda* leaving the press.

Our manifestos, like theirs, demanded what every manifesto demands: the abolishment of the world as we know it. But what turned us on was the revolution itself, not its possible success. Inevitably, the world as we knew it was abolished. It was abolished each new morning a little until it got to be about 1984 and then it was so abolished only nostalgia recognized it. Rosa Luxemburg had tried to reconcile her personal life with her politics, but it didn't work because at the time the two languages had far too few points in common. By the time *we* inked our stencils the languages of politics and self were locked in wars of articulation and had far too many rhetorical places in common. I say "rhetorical" because the reality underneath much of the speech about "love," "armed love," "unarmed love"—that would be the Venus de Milo—belied humongous and inexpressible anxieties that gave birth to whole political movements of their own, most importantly, feminism.

The two revolutions in my poem, the sexy and the techy, have come to pass. Not only that: they have merged. In 1974 sex and technology were enemies. It was people against machines then. That was the simple faith that animated sexual revolutionaries: the mongolian cluster fuck against the state's megacomputer. The suits at keyboards against the nude vegetarians. Of course, even then, the truth of the matter was that the sexual revolution was made possible in large part by technology. Dr. Carl Djerassi, who synthesized the first oral contraceptive, is a friend of mine. He has quite an exalted idea of his discovery, the formula for which he has placed among the primary acts of creation painted on his ceiling in San Francisco. Another prime mover of the sexual revolution was Dr. Albert Hoffman, the discoverer of LSD, who provided the cosmic key without which this revolution would not have been possible.

Nonetheless, most rank-and-file revolutionaries, us horny twelve-year-olds, denied and obscured our prime movers because to acknowledge them would have necessitated dealing with the inhuman particulars, which are well-known enemies of faith. The inhuman particulars, at close range, were woven into the very texture of our fleeting liberty, which was, for the most part, imaginary. To oppose imagination to the whole monolith of reality takes a great deal of faith and energy. What made our faith bearable was its capacity to generate paradox and irony. I saw, most of the time anyway, the contradictions and absurdities of our revolution, which was intended, precisely, to cleanse us of the pain of living. Contradictions are tonic, paradox is a kind of purgative, and irony provides scar tissue. This I call "imaginary medicine" and it worked very well on the frontline wounds of the sex war. Later came AIDS and, while it didn't make imaginary medicine obsolete, it posed certain technological questions, including some ontological ones that gave our seventies "body without organs" a whole new form. AIDS reformed and reformatted the body to bring it in line with the counter-revolution of the eighties and nineties. AIDS is a Republican disease.

While we are still in my poem, in 1974—I hate to leave those pleasant days—let me pause for a moment on the political revolutionaries who existed in a universe parallel to ours though they often inhabited the same pads and, sometimes, the same bodies. The politicos, as I remember them, seemed to me notoriously incapable of grasping paradox, possibly because they lacked a sense of humor. They were taken seriously only by the FBI, which, likewise, lacked the elementary organ of humor. These twin bummers, politicos and their fuzz brothers, acted or rather reenacted the shadow ideological quarrels of the 1930s, unaware of the fact that the languages of the ideologies they invested with such magic powers had in fact been emptied of meaning. I was possibly more conscious of the bankruptcy of ideological discourses than many of my contemporaries because I grew up under a Red totalitarianism that used all the buzzwords of community and liberty but meant exactly the opposite by them.

The speeches of Communist bureaucrats were pure white noise to my generation by the midsixties, just as the patriotic and jingoistic blather of official American culture meant nothing to young Americans. When the so-called new left took over the regurgitated gruel of pseudo-Marxism they condemned themselves to instant obsolescence and became useful, as I've said, only to the police. They were very useful to the police, however, who would have had to invent them if they didn't exist. Thanks to the so-called political radicals of that decade—well into the midseventies—the state's repressive apparatus flourished and came down hard on everybody else. They didn't succeed in destroying our ongoing paradoxical revolution because by its very nature our revolution abolished itself whenever it got a chance. Only revolutions that overarticulate themselves can be overthrown. And, whatever else sexual revolutionaries might be accused of, overarticulation was not one of our sins, a situation due in part to the paucity of the vocabulary of joy and its unselfconscious nonverbal nature. We failed only insofar as we made successful translations.

These approaches to revolution reenacted, on a wider scale, the opposition between Leninism and Dadaism in 1920s Europe. The famous—apocryphal—photograph of Lenin playing chess with Tristan Tzara in a Zurich café is emblematic of that opposition. Poised over the chessboard of history are two revolutionaries: the notorious Dadaist who gave form to a new mind-set with paradox and self-abolition at its center, and the Russian Bolshevik who would give shape to the world for the remainder of the century. The Swiss police were much more suspicious of Tzara the Dadaist who staged incomprehensible provocations in public than of the studious Russian who mostly kept to himself. They were mistaken at the time because Lenin proved to be the more influential player, but now, after Leninism is gone, Dada is still with us, having proven itself to be a permanent approach to the society of consumption and spectacle.

Between Tzara and Lenin, Rosa Luxemburg stands as an exemplary model of failure, and I say this in praise because failure is one of the virtues in my book. Rosa was a disciplined professional revolutionary who saw the pitfalls of discipline and the beauty of chaos, which was her vision of social democracy. She was also a traditional romantic who struggled with the bourgeois conventions without escaping them. She could have never accepted the radical refusal of Dada because she was an optimist, one of a long line of messianic Jewish spirits invested in eschatology, the science of "the end." And she could not approve of Lenin's undemocratic Communist Party centralism because it resembled all too closely the autocratic tsarist empire in which she was born. She mirrored the struggle, too, between two currents of Jewish thought, the rational and the mystical, exemplified in her time by Zionism, with its socialist roots, and Hasidism, which was rooted in ecstasy and unmediated knowledge of God.

On the surface, the world we live in, the so-called western democracy, looks very much like Rosa Luxemburg's vision: a functioning social democracy with eschatological anxieties that struggles against bourgeois conventions with the aid, ironically, of late capitalism. The fact that capitalism, not socialism, turned out to be the revolutionary force, par excellence, is an irony that would not have surprised Luxemburg, who must have believed, with Marx and Engels, that

> The bourgeoisie cannot exist without constantly revolutionising the instruments of production, and thereby the relations of production, and with them the whole relations of society. . . . All fixed, fast-frozen relations, with their train of ancient and venerable prejudices and opinions are swept away, all new-formed ones become antiquated before they can ossify. All that is solid melts into the air, all that is holy is profaned, and man is at last compelled to face his real conditions of life, and his mutual relations with a sober eye.

Pretty groovy, no? But state socialism, whose authoritarian form just gave up the ghost, was a defender of conservatism and an enemy of revolution, whether bourgeois or any other kind. Suffice it to note that to Stalin, the family was "the basis of society," and to Hitler, the national socialist, "The family is the smallest but most valuable unit in the complete structure of the state." And you can put Dan Quayle's family values in that company, too.

But how about this? "The bourgeoisie has torn away from the family its sentimental veil, and has reduced the family relation to a mere money relation." That's from *The Communist Manifesto*, as published by Karl Marx and Friedrich Engels in 1888. Is this good or bad? Well, in the first version of the *Manifesto*, before censorship by the Communist League, the second demand of the revolution after "the abolition of private property" was "the abolition of the family." Marx saw the family as an extension of private property where man owns woman, couple own children.

The socialisms of our time completely erased Marx's first thought and defended, until the moment of their own erasure, the status quo of gender inequality and bourgeois marriage. Within only four years of the collapse of Red totalitarian regimes in Eastern Europe and the ex-USSR, before the economic situation even changed significantly, capitalism has already wreaked havoc with those societies, causing experimentation, fragmentation, alienation, atomization, and destruction of traditional bonds. Happening in the middle of economic collapse and famine these changes are not buoyant but depressing. The collapse of the pseudo-Marxist ideology has produced a deep depression that is far from the exhilarated alienation of Westerners.

In the U.S., the sex revolution of the late sixties to the midseventies was a triumph of capitalism at a time of plenty. Our revolution certified consumption because it created an appetite for luxury, a cult of youth and beauty that created new markets, and an existential despair that demanded palliatives and substitutes, leading to the current intense markets in virtual realities. The sex revolution exhausted reality and caused a voracious consumer demand for alternative worlds. A graffito in the Haight in the eighties, quoted by Paul Krassner in his auto-biography, says it all: "Love is Revenue." Any number of sexual revolutions—or any other kinds of utopias for that matter—can be man-ufactured now, if one doesn't mind the texture of the simulacrum, which is only slightly different anyway and infused with instant amnesia.

In the 1990s in the West, sex is in bed with technology. And only with technology. Each one of us is partnered with a machine. You may think that you are in a relationship with another human being, but you are not. The alter ego that responds to your reflexes is a technological de-vice. This is true without exception, therefore only machines have re-lationships. Furthermore, you are a machine, subject to complete control by the inhuman center of a mechanical discourse that extorts whatever energy you have left by dividing your liberty into smaller and smaller increments.

Gender politics, minority rights politics, labor politics, and most politics politics in our time are completely invested in the smooth func-tioning of the production-consumption machine that is capable of pro-ducing equality, equity, justice, and love. Consumption is color-blind and gender-blind and it can even produce the illusion of difference by maintaining or inventing faux-gender, faux-class, faux-race distinc-tions. The only thing the P.C. machine cannot do is to renew the re-sources from which it draws its energy: human liberty and the planet body. Those are the raw materials needed to fulfill and overfulfill the demand for utopia.

In the West, the technological revolution has assimilated the human revolution. Or, in theological terms, you can say that God regained con-trol of his rebellious creations. Or that the capitalist state won. Now, at the end of the century, everybody's institutionalized: everyone is either in prison, in school, or in a mental hospital. The sexual revolution has become a "revolution" between quotation marks—available on MTV, video, CD-ROM, virtual reality, or, close to the edge, in wetproof body sheathing.

Now and then, you see some grizzled twelve-year-olds, clutching their bottles of Ripple with gnarled fingers around a trash-can fire. Their fellow travelers glare down at them from their high-rise suites while their machines fuck them. Losers are always those who keep the faith past closing time, but at least they aren't getting screwed by their expanding data base. When a revolution becomes the plaything of a data base, any number of things happen, but the main one is that one loses touch with the untamed desire of the dispossessed. While the former revolutionaries are being virtually sexed by their digital masters, the inarticulate energy gathers at the edges. Rock 'n' roll.

Carl **Djerassi**'s

Cosmogony

My friend Carl Djerassi synthesized the first oral contraceptive, a.k.a. The Birth Control Pill. On the ceiling of his penthouse in San Francisco there is a Michelangelo-like fresco featuring poets, Dante and Blake among them, flying in with their golden verses trailing behind. They are coming in from the right side of the heavens: reaching out to meet them from the left heavens, like the Hand of God, is the formula for the birth control pill. Only the Pope might fail to see the humor of this, but then the Pope would think that Dr. Djerassi is the Devil.

Dr. Djerassi *looks* like the Devil: he has a limp and tufty eyebrows, two classic features of the Devil from Beelzebub to Mephistopheles. He also collects art and writes fiction, which is full-time deviltry for the ones in the know. One would think that the good doctor might rest on his laurels. But no. Together with Dr. Stanley Leibo, he has now proposed collecting and freezing the sperm of the United States Armed Forces in order to study sperm longevity. Should this study prove that sperm can be frozen for long periods of time, men could go undergo vasectomies en masse, certain that any time they wanted children they could just draw on their account.

The social consequences of this would be equivalent to those of the birth-control pill. The pill gave women a choice and it initiated the so-called sexual revolution, which means that women were able to enjoy sex without fear for the first time in their gender's history. That freedom would now be available to men, who would no longer be victims of accidents and unwanted children. The long-term survival of sperm could also insure the possibility of having children after death, if the survivors decided that it would be a good idea. One could, for instance, father the offspring of one's grandchildren. Should this succeed, Dr. Djerassi can lay claim to the right side of heaven as well: all those poets would be retroactively justified for having made so much of love.

I Met Miss America

I met Miss America. She was nice. And she was cold. We were seated before paparazzi at an outdoor table in Hollywood. She was wearing a wool coat. Still, she was shivering. She leaned right up against me and shivered some more. "Good coat," I said, meaning that it looked thick enough to me so that she shouldn't have been cold. "Thank you," she said. I hadn't meant "beautiful coat." I meant "good coat." But I let it slide.

You have to feel sorry for Miss America. She's nineteen years old and every night she has to be in a different town to tell people that she's against hunger and homelessness. In a way, she's hungry and homeless herself. She was shivering just like the homeless because she spent every night at a different temperature in a different motel room. And she was hungry because every time it was her turn to eat, someone asked her something so she never got anything into her mouth. Plus, she has to watch her figure.

When I was a kid I used to think that Miss America was the President's wife. Now I know better.

On this particular night she got to eat even less because we were at a banquet for Oxfam America, an outfit that feeds people, and 60 percent of the people there, including Miss America, got to eat only a few grains of rice with dirty water. About 15 percent got some beans and tortillas, and the rest got a gourmet meal and wine. Your randomly drawn door ticket decided what you ate. Miss America and I, we were in the 60 percent. That's how the world eats and Oxfam was making the point to Hollywood stars who seemed only too happy to lie around the floor eating dirty rice. They too have figures to keep. At the gourmet tables, the privileged scarfed down pâté. I started singing the "Internationale," hoping to spark a minirevolution, but my fellow grubbers weren't interested. They wanted their lesson. A couple of kids came down to hand their salads to us but I refused. "Let's eat the kids instead," I suggested to no avail. Miss America took the salad, though. "This is what it's all about," she beamed. No kidding.

Fairy-**Tale** Sports **Babes**

Everybody was disappointed that Tonya Harding didn't win an Olympic medal. We wanted her to win and then we wanted her to be found guilty. That's the American way: reward and punish. We want our heroes to win at all cost and then we want to punish them for it. And when they've been punished we write country songs about them.

Tonya is the perfect country-song gal: she smokes cigarettes, shoots pool, dances topless, and may or may not have done what we think she did. Half the men in America want to go out with her. But then, they are writing letters to Lorena Bobbit, too.

By comparison, Nancy Kerrigan is Snow White, and while Tonya Harding may not be the Wicked Witch, we find Snow White a little boring. She *is* the fairest of them all and has great style but in the presence of such perfection we are all dwarves.

They both seem awfully cool to me: there is so much cold, cold cash riding on them, it's hard to know where the ice stops and the hype starts.

This winter there were great snowstorms, ice storms, and howling winds. The world seemed to turn to ice and, appropriately, we had our winter's fairy tale. I wish we had as much enthusiasm for the suffering of real people freezing in places like Sarajevo, site of the 1984 Olympics. But that's not a fairy tale, not the American kind, anyway.

New **Penal** Penalties

Let's face it: penises have come to dominate our national debate with an intensity previously reserved for hair.

Hair, you may remember, preoccupied our collective psyche for two decades, dividing all Americans into those who didn't have any and those who had a lot.

Penises are to the nineties what hair was to the sixties—thanks to Bobbit's bobber, Michael Jackson's bad, and now the President's Jones. Penises are now dividing Americans into those who have them and those who don't.

Those who don't are doing their best to expose those who do. Lorena Bobbit and Paula Jones, with help from the press, are the latest generators of penile images to the general public. The groundwork has, of course, been laid by Senators Kennedy, Hart, and Packwood. But, somehow, those senators' troubles weren't quite as graphic.

How did we get such pictorial clarity here? The transition was provided, I believe, by the pubic hairs invoked during the Clarence Thomas confirmation hearings. That image was reinforced by Michael Jackson's crotch-grabbing gesture on TV before millions of Americans. Shortly after that, the ostensible object of grabbing surfaced in the headlines, accused of varied crimes.

Madonna and Roseanne replicated Jackson's gesture, but while briefly newsworthy, their demonstrations lacked weight. It was only after Lorena Bobbit gave us the charming image of state troopers crawling on a dark highway looking for her severed spousal *objet* that America focused firmly.

In the sixties, the hair curtain that fell between generations eclipsed the Iron and Bamboo Curtains. Eventually, those with a lot of hair edged out the hairless, but by that time they started losing their hair and were bereft of their youth and its symbol. Hair was a symbol of potency, but time is a Delilah.

I pray and hope that the same fate does not await penises. What if those who have them win at just about the time they begin to lose their reason for having them? What can possibly succeed the penis?

Of course, there may not be much difference between the sixties and the nineties. Hair was just another word for penis, too. And baldness was just another word for nothing left to lose. We were so prudish and naive back then. We meant penis, but we said hair. And we had so much more to lose. Now we say penis, but we mean no penis.

Whose side is time on, anyway?

Honeymoon in Budapest

I would have kept my two cents to myself on the union between Michael and Lisa Marie—not wanting to add to the river of zingers already flooding the nation—but when they decided to honeymoon in Budapest I couldn't resist. That's my turf, and the idea of the combined Jackson and Presley unit digging the Danube at dusk took my breath away.

Some cynics have suggested that Michael needed some potent proof of heterosexuality and there could be none better than marrying the King's daughter. But even if that were true, what's Lisa Marie getting out of it? She doesn't have to be anybody's alibi. She may have been Michael's good friend and friends do things for each other, like marrying for a visa. But in this case, either one could have paid a hundred girls to say "I do" to Michael. Liz Taylor would have done it in a second. She may have even offered, but Michael might have felt a little peculiar being Liz's fortieth husband.

Anyway, this is all speculation and it detracts from the main thing, which is Michael and Lisa Marie strolling hand in hand over the bridges of Budapest, gawking at the ghosts of furious Turks and Soviets who have failed to hold that splendid city. Michael is, of course, aware of this history. He was filming a video in which he rescues a generic Communist state from Red army troops. Now, it's a little late for that, but if Michael wants to save the world from Communism again it's his prerogative. For his money—and now Lisa Marie's—he can bring Communism back and then topple it as many times as he wants. The point is that such a macho man was never yet seen on earth. Forget Superman. Forget Schwarzenegger. Michael has bypassed them by miles.

He married the King's daughter and is single-handedly toppling the world's worst tyranny. Who can say anything bad about him? And if you do, he's already said it himself. Bad. Bad. As for Lisa Marie, she is the real mystery. In my opinion, Elvis, her dad, is alive. He's best friends with Michael. *He* gave him Lisa Marie. And she obeyed. Because she's a good girl. Good. Good. That's Bad and Good. In Budapest. Together.

POSTSCRIPT: The cynics were right. Bad. Bad. Poor Elvis.

The **End** of the **World** (Again)

The End of the World was supposed to come in September 1994, according to Harold Camping, a radio evangelist. A rabbi named Isser Weisberg thought so, too. The comet that slammed into Jupiter was their cue.

Frankly, I'm getting tired of this. I've now sat through several ends of the world, most notably about ten years ago in San Francisco. Everyone reclined in Golden Gate Park getting high, waiting for the stars to kill us as the astrologers said they would. It was horrible to have to go home after the world didn't end. It was embarrassing. The things did and said while waiting came hauntingly back. I remembered telling a total stranger stuff I wouldn't tell an evangelist, a rabbi, *or* a bartender. That's the worst part about the end of the world: surviving it.

For the last two decades scores of eschatologists, from high to low, have proclaimed the end of everything. The End of History. The End of Literacy. The End of Cities. The End of People. The End of Communism. That happened, but then it came back. The End of Philosophy, which all these ends seemed to be about in one way or another, was proclaimed by Deconstructionists until the End of Deconstruction which was proclaimed by Post-Deconstructionists.

In response, Derrida, the most famous Deconstructionist still alive is out there deconstructing the very idea of Death, which is to say that he's proclaiming the End of the End. The End of the World and the End of Everything is such big business they've got William Burroughs to do advertising. That really *is* the end. Burroughs has been America's chief cultural undertaker for three decades. When he shows up, you know it's serious. And you know that everything *did* end.

History's just a jumbled heap. Cities are ghostly. Or ghastly. Nobody reads. Especially not philosophy. And all those Golden Gate waiters have no memory left. And you can see the wires in what used to be people. The trouble with the emperor's new clothes now is that everybody knows they don't exist and, still, they want some just like them. This is a new kind of thing and it signals, in my opinion, the end of this riff. It came, see?

Armageddon to Some

T he people eagerly awaiting Armageddon, from religious fundamentalists to paranoid Nazis, have no choice but to wish a fiery end. They've been such failures in this world only the end of it can justify their miserable, creepy existence. The fact is that their world *has* already ended, a long time ago, despite their protophilosophy's occasional spurts of life. The apparent strength of fanatics from Iran to Michigan is no more than the jerky motions of a corpse animated by electric shocks.

The God buried by Nietzsche in the last century found scores of other gods in that grave: one of humanity's best tricks is the invention and disposal of gods. But gods do not go quietly: ideally they would like to take every living thing with them. Their afterdeaths are stormy. The rush to divide God's legacy pits those who would take the virtues of kindness and righteous living against those who Bible-thump for vengeance and the Apocalypse.

One whole century of science but not progress has gone by since the old bearded guy was pronounced *kaput*. Our tools have outstripped by far any psychological improvement. The insanity of Hitler's Germans half a century ago is a perfect example of what can be done by technically competent people steeped in murky Nordic fairy tales, twilight sentimentality, kitsch culture, and medieval Christianity. If the baby Nazis in Michigan or the bearded baby mullahs were armed only with slingshots they would be no more dangerous than mosquitoes. The trouble is that their peashooters are atomic. This wasn't the case with the followers of Baal or Jupiter or Vishnu, who could cause only limited damage.

Germany may have been militarily defeated in World War II, but the hunger for simple explanations and the anger that drove national-socialism lives on. Of course, it's easier to believe, as Pat Robertson or Colonel Olson do, that a Masonic-Jewish conspiracy rules the world, than to try to figure out where the pictures on their TV really come from. It's easier to end the world than to learn it. If we want to stem the tide of violence swelling from such ignorance, we must engage in some vigorous battles to demystify the paranoid delusions on which the hateful feed. The time has come to disarm the dead gods.

The Ten Commandments

I once met a guy on the bus who told me, "I left a Bible in a motel in Hollywood and now they are making a movie from the parts I underlined." The man who found that Bible is, it turns out, Cecil B. DeMille, and the movie he made is *The Ten Commandments.* And around Easter every year, the old warhorse gets trotted out on TV.

It's a reliable measuring stick of what was, is, and will be. God, for one, is one tough dude in this picture: He spews plagues, kills children, and starves people for every infraction. He expresses himself with purple death fogs that are a lot like poison gas, parting seas, and bloody rivers, exactly as if he were Cecil B. DeMille, whom He maybe was. But at least He still talks to people, which after a while, He stopped doing, leaving His actions open to speculation.

God also looked askance on girlie shows, of which we are given two memorable examples: the Busby Berkeley–style aerobics performed before the Pharaoh, Yul Brynner, and the Bedouin tent dance performed before Moses, Charlton Heston. There is also some Mardi Gras–style frolicking around the Golden Calf but it's been tastefully reduced to running around in circles spritzing wine and rose petals at a tied-up virgin screaming "Shame!"

God, of course, likes his people to talk aphoristically, so they say things like: "So it is told. So it will be written," which may be Cecil's greatest contribution to Pidgin English.

In the end, God's people, under the leadership of blue-eyed, red-haired, bare-chested Hebrews, get out of bondage with the tablets on which the Ten Commandments have been written very slowly by God in a language that doesn't resemble Hebrew, with a pen of fire.

Incidentally, blue-eyed, red- or flaxen-haired Hebrews escaped from this movie and ended up on the murals in the Mormon Temple in Salt Lake City where they climb the walls, depicting the same story. Now— if only that guy on the bus would start underlining *The Critique of Pure Reason.*

History

H istory is no place for the faint of heart. It's full of hidden intentions, unforeseen results, and above all, bodies. If history were a well you could look into you'd reel in horror. It's full of bodies and it stinks.

Now, thanks to the *National Standards of World History* issued by the government for grades five through twelve, the teaching of history is as nightmarish as the real thing. These National Standards, subtitled *Exploring Paths to the Present,* have been criticized by various ideologues as evincing the hidden agenda of multiculturalists. But even if this were true, which, in my opinion, it is not, that's not what makes these "standards" a nightmare. Opening the book almost anywhere, one finds, for instance, that your ninth-grader should be able to

> Demonstrate understanding of the emergence of Islam and how Islam spread in Southwest Asia, North Africa, and Europe . . . by analyzing the political, social, and religious problems confronting the Byzantine and Sassanid Persian Empires in the seventh century and the commercial role of Arabia in the Southwest Asian economy.

Our ninth-grader is bid in parenthesis to accomplish this by analyzing "multiple causation." Right. But if your child is only in fifth grade he or she can accomplish the same result by merely "describing the life of Muhammad, the development of the early Muslim community, and the basic teachings and practices of Islam." Yeah, cool, that's a lot easier.

A little later, we find our ninth-grader encouraged to "write a series of newspaper accounts of the Indian uprising of 1857." And if he or she has any time after that, how about "preparing some arguments for why the empress dowager originally supported the Boxer Rebellion."

By the time our high-schooler has explored the "paths to the present," he or she has given up any hope of going to Lollapalooza or seeing Smashing Pumpkins at the Superdome. I'm not against history but I believe that this is why the empress dowager supported the Boxer Rebellion in the first place.

Hair, Part Nine

They made a fuss over President Clinton's haircut, which snarled airport traffic in Los Angeles for a while. This is not as trivial as his mostly bald opponents would like America to think. Mr. Clinton has hair, and that's a fact.

Once upon a time he had even more hair. That was when America was divided into two classes: people with long hair and people with crew cuts. The so-called generation gap was a hair gap, between people who hated the Vietnam War and said so with hair, and people who loved the war and clipped their heads to prove it. What really irks the folks about the President's hair is that the Iron Curtain is gone but hair is here to stay.

During the campaign there was a lot of fuss about Hillary Rodham

Clinton's hair, another battle of generational symbols. Mrs. Clinton's headbanded hair was nothing short of a war cry to the hairmongers of America. Eventually, she fell in line somewhat with the diffuse, style-fuzzy status quo of the nineties.

It used to be said that politics was a male province conducted mostly in saloons, but in the nineties the debate has moved from the saloons to the salons. The saloons elected Ronald Reagan, whose pompadour and pomade reminded people of a time when men were men and women wore hair nets. The radical hair revolt of the 1960s, which started with rock 'n' roll, caused too many hairy changes for most voters.

It is said that an average person has 90,000 to 140,000 hair follicles, which is about as many hairs as there are votes in a medium-sized town. Most Americans live in small to medium-sized towns so it follows that they vote with their hair. When they don't vote with their feet, that is. I'm sorry. I digress.

The point is that the politics of hair is as important as politics proper, and that as the millennium approaches, there will be new hair wars between the hair-haves and the hairless. The electorate has a hair trigger when it comes to the top of the head.

It's a **Crime**!

few campaigns ago most political candidates were scared to say "crime" because everyone knew that the word stood for "blacks." But now, in the blessed new day of right-wing America, the word *crime* is being shouted from the rooftops. It still means blacks but the politicians don't care anymore: blacks and their fellow travelers, the liberals, are a fair target. The poor and their partisans are the newest Commies. Even the old and—I thought—discredited IQ test is making a comeback, to provide a "scientific" base for raging racism.

We are a country of recurrent fads: unabashed bashing of the poor is one of the most recurrent. It is usually followed by economic depression for *everyone*. And then the true values that make a community—

not the false ones that make up right-wing rhetoric—are bound to come back: compassion and rage at the real culprits. And the real culprits, I'm not sorry to say, are the very people who make the most noise about crime. The issue keeps them in business.

It also keeps in business the industry of fear that funds them: the gun dealers, the security companies, the secured-building builders, the new-jail contractors, the health-care operators, and the insurance companies. Crime, as Marx once said, keeps the judges and lawyers in business, too.

The only thing new since Marx said that is the media, which couldn't exist these days without crime. Everything, from news to vérité shows, from soaps to movies, trades in crime. Americans love crime. We love our criminals on TV and at the movies and we even love to elect them, provided that they are big enough criminals.

We believe that Oliver North, who nearly overthrew constitutional government, is electable, whereas a two-bit crack dealer ought to be executed. The CIA drug business is still classified, but a street junkie has barely any rights. There are one million people in jail in the U.S.A. and that's big business, too. Verily, as Poincaré said, the scale is the phenomenon. Crime is as vital to the current candidate as air: if the petty hood was suddenly suppressed, somebody'd pay him to reappear. The right wing couldn't live a day without its criminals.

The **Sound** of the **Body** Politic

The body politic these days sounds like a heavy metal band tuning up in a Quonset hut. It hasn't been this loud and harsh since Richard Nixon played on "Watergate," a show I used to watch every day. Even the cold warriors' yelps of glee when Communism collapsed about a thousand years ago didn't sound this loud and screechy.

It all begins in the morning with people like columnist Cal Thomas jumping out of the paper like a cat on fire. Such howls of anguish! This particular day Cal is screaming about how unfair the world is to Dick Armey for calling Barney Frank Barney Fag. It could have been worse, wails Cal. Like how? If he'd called him Barbie Fag? What if somebody'd called Dick Armey, Army Dick? Would Cal still scream?

After all that noise, you turn to the plain news, hoping for dignified quiet. The President has proposed to raise the minimum wage from where it was in the seventies to something that will buy a roast, let's say, if you work for a week. Nice, quiet idea. But then the screaming starts. It's the Republicans: they don't want the minimum wage raised. And they don't want welfare either.

Then what is it they want, you may ask. If you don't work they won't let you live; if you do work, you can't live on what they pay you. Maybe they want to kill all the poor people. Maybe that's why they scream so loud. They figure if everyone's deaf it's easier to kill them. Oh, is there any quiet spot?

The arts used to be a nice respite from the clang and drang of men in sweaty suits with overarticulate points of view. You'd look at a painting, watch a ballet, and achieve serenity. But wouldn't you know it? Where the painting used to be there is a discolored space with the warning:

TAX-PAID FILTH WAS REMOVED FROM HERE. WATCH FOR MARKET-PRODUCED FAMILY VALUE ART COMING TO THIS SPACE IN THE NEXT CENTURY.

And then you figure it out—the din, the bleating, the shrieks: it's the market. The nation's become a big open-air market with everybody bidding for soon-to-be-unemployed politicians. That's what all the racket's about.

Pizza Woes

Congress and people are in a cutting-and-banning mood. You hear this all the time now. Today I thought I'd do my part and try to find something to ban and cut. I see in the paper that a boy in Miami shot a man for wanting an extra slice from the pizza the boy bought for some homeless people, including the greedy man. Charity was mixed up, in this kid, with a heightened sense of justice. I've always been leery of charity for that reason: it's just bait, usually.

I also see that in California a pizza thief got twenty-five-years-to-life. That's not quite getting killed but it's still pretty severe. That's about five years a slice. I bet the man's sorry he didn't go for the poached salmon in ginger sauce with the steamed vegetables instead.

Not so long ago, two Eskimo kids were banished to two remote islands for robbing a pizza delivery man. The price for pizza-snatching is going up and up.

There was a time, back in the old days, when the national food was hamburger, not pizza. Everything was better then. Nobody snatched anybody's burger because it was disgusting eating a burger with a bite taken out of it. It's not like detaching a slice. The burger was also made of just three things, brown meat, bun, and slop, not a hundred different layers of things that can vary. The burger was simple to grasp, unlike the pizza which is complex and multicultural. And while both burger and pizza are round, the burger is an individual sphere, while the pizza is a communal circle. It is astounding that after the collapse of Communism it should be the Communistic pizza and not the individualistic burger that's got a hold on the nation.

The answer is clear: ban pizza. It makes people insane. It is slicing through the moral fiber of the nation like a razor-edged Frisbee with pepperoni on it.

Japanese
Comedians

N ews comes from Japan that two
comedians have been elected governors of Tokyo and Osaka. This could
be bad news for the markets because Japanese humor is not like ours.

My friend Janet worked for a while on this Japanese TV show called
something like "Where Are You?" The idea was to blindfold the con-
testants and fly them to some famous place. Once there, the blindfolds
are removed and they get to answer the question: "Where are you?"
If they guess right, they get a car or a radio or something. But if they
are wrong, they get punished. In this particular episode, the contes-
tants had their blindfolds removed on Bourbon Street in New Orleans.
Most of them knew where they were, but one guy didn't. "Punishment!
Punishment!"

The loser was taken to a Bourbon Street bar that specializes in those horrid alcoholic concoctions with seven different kinds of booze in them, plus raw eggs and cane sugar. The producer held the ignoramus's head on the bar while the bartender mixed the drink listing the ingredients out loud: "Gin, rum, vodka, raw egg, vanilla, brown sugar, etc." He then poured this evil thing down the guy's throat and afterward the guy had to recall all the ingredients: "Gin, rum, vodka, egg, sugar, etc." Notice I'm not doing Judge Ito here. Anyway, if he remembered everything, fine. If he didn't, it was head back on the bar again and a brand-new mixed drink down the gullet. This was repeated till he got it right.

Now imagine this technique applied to government. If the people perform their civic duties, no problem. If they don't, out come the bulldozers and wreck the house and garden. If Japanese producers manage to keep cars and apples out of Japan, fine. If not, here come those big spanking paddles, ouch, ouch. Of course, I may be wrong about this, because that's how government works everywhere: you pay the taxes, okay. You no pay taxes, go to the pokey. Which means, of course, that government always had a Japanese sense of humor, and that their comedians are ahead of ours in politics. We still elect bad dramatic actors.

The **Dog** with the **Chip** in His **Neck**

Part 2

The **Dog** with the **Chip** in His **Neck**

Sherri Wigdore, who works for Intelligent Electronics, has a dog with a computer chip in his neck. The dog's name is Zena. Sherri's dog Zena is a big dog, of the kind known as Bouviers, and if that wasn't enough, nobody can remove the chip from Zena's neck because it's been injected there by a vet. A veterinarian, that is, not an ex-soldier. If Zena is lost somewhere like on a ski slope, let's say, whoever finds him can take him to an office where they scan his neck and retrieve all his vital data, like "This is Zena, Sherri's dog, Internet address, azena/@/AOL.comm." There is a central data bank somewhere that has all the data contained on all the computer chips in the necks of all the dogs in America. When Zena's scanned, this data bank fires down the info.

Sherri told me this while showing me the latest computer techne on the floor of the New Orleans Superdome. A computer named Bob can record your voice and transcribe your words on the screen. At first, it's a bit unsteady. You say "Sherri's dog Zena," and it writes "SHEEDO-ZINA," which is the Russian translation. Apparently, it takes a while for Bob to learn your accent and vocabulary. You know how it is. But then Bob not only learns how you talk and how you say it, it anticipates what you have to say. Eventually, it interrupts you because it knows how you say it better than you're about to say it.

After about a week, you don't need to talk at all: Bob does all your talking and it writes down what it says for you. But get this: after another week you can have a chip put in your neck that allows Bob to read your mind wherever you are, even on a ski slope trying to deal with a lost dog. Bob will put your neck chip in touch with Zena's neck chip and the two chips will lead you to the vet. Give the system a few weeks and nobody will ever be lost again. And to be a chip in somebody's neck will be the highest compliment.

Voice **Mail** or the **Terror** of the **Impersonal**

I've been a Luddite ever since my encounter at age ten with a bad public telephone. The thing ate my coin and I kicked it. Money started pouring out, but this gift turned sour when a policeman nabbed me and accused me of being a hoodlum.

Since then, I have seen phones terrorize human beings with increasing frequency. At first, they were just these black harbingers of bad news. Gradually, they began to dominate our lives. First, they detached themselves from walls and became portable. Then they made us believe that talking to someone was just like seeing them. No need for the awesome and terrifying complexity of face-to-face encounters. So we began to see a lot less of each other and entrust ourselves blindly to the yak-yak evermore.

But until recently they still required us humans at both ends. Then came the answering machine, which made it possible to talk to someone without the inconvenience of being interrupted. That eliminated one human. Not long after, the message machines started talking to one another. That dispensed with the need to have voice-to-voice encounters. Recently, I picked up and a someone on the other end said, evidently disappointed: "I was hoping to speak with your answering machine." "Sorry," I said, and hung up so he could. I actually felt guilty, as if I had intruded on some newly privileged reality.

But in the ever-quickening now even tape-messaging with its residual humanness has been eliminated. On the other end of your intended communication, you are met by a machine brain that speaks to you without allowing you to reply: *Press One If . . .* , and then *Press One Inside That If . . .* , and *If You Press Three Inside That . . . If you will have less than a second to begin again, Press One, If, If, If. . . . One, two, one, two!* The chilling mechanical being is giving you your marching orders.

The Luddites, you may remember, were English workers in the nineteenth century who smashed the machines that took away their jobs. Just think how they would have reacted to machines that took away their *voices!* They would have *powdered* them!

The **Talking** Cure
Becomes the Talking
Virus

We are becoming more emotionally dead and increasingly more blasé about what we hear and watch. Maybe we consume the increasingly grotesque confessional shows à la Ricky Lake and all because we are losing the habit of spontaneous intimacy with each other. So we prefer to watch the sorrows of TV ghosts. They are just a little less painful than our couch mates. All those freaks make us feel NORMAL—but we are not. We are consumers of freakishness possessed of exhibitionist envy. Sooner or later everyone will want to empty his or her closets for the chance of being a five-second demon on national TV. These shows are not about therapy: they are peddlers of psychological crack. Americans are now addicted to these confessional orgies and like all addicts we crave higher and higher doses.

Mere murderers and rapists no longer suffice. I'm sure people call the networks all the time trying to one-up last night's sleazebag.

What do the networks do? Rate the freaks on a ONE-TO-TEN scale? Ten if you're a serial killer, one if you're a mere rapist? Secretly, every TV watcher dreams of being something loathsome enough to be on "Geraldo." You can say our imagination's been stimulated. Even as our national psyche's getting a hole in it the size of the national debt.

You'd think that the nation's closets would be empty by now. We used to lie on talking couches and talk to therapists. We still do—only we aren't talking. We just lie there. The TV is our big, bad talking couch now.

Head **Full** of Numbers

I was flying through cyberspace, light as a feather, the other day, when this government zit with a mug full of glitches, asks to see my numbers, as if I am a real human being, not just a byte off his virtual log. Now I don't normally carry human numbers, street name and digits, fax, phone, beeper, e-mail, zip code, bar code, credit digits, SS number, security codes, and the like when I go info-cruising, so it was really annoying.

It reminded me of something from the age of street patrols when people used to go out. Or something from the age of the couch potato when the slogan was, "It's not Big Brother watching. We *are* Big Brother, *watching!*" That, naturally, came after "Big Brother is watching" and all the encryption fights, which really had more to do with Big Brother listening. And before that, it was "Big Brother wants you!," which was the last time he was so polite about his needs and wants.

Before that, there was nothing. I mean, just people. That's all: people writing in longhand to other people far away. It was faster to walk there directly. Letters took years. But now, here is this imaginary cop slowing down my imaginary cruise and he wants my human numbers, which, even if I knew where they were, would be absolutely of no use. Everyone has a secret bar code now. I don't know my bar-code number just as he doesn't know his.

This is our shared secret in the disembodied world where we spend our nonexistence. We are not dead: it's just that we don't have bodies, numbers, or memory. We have a directional imperative but it's not geographical or psychological. We can go toward or into any dimension as long as we move. And we can only move if we desire to move, which is what the imperative is, I guess. So, here I am, I have no idea how to respond to this law officer I have created out of my own desire to be censured. Perhaps I want my imperative censured. I don't know. I'm keying this in longhand.

The **Computer** to the **After**life, or **Put** the **Fingers** Back in

Digital

The lovely headline in my local paper says it all: NIGHTMARES DOG COMPUTER JUNKIES. It's all there: Nightmares. Computers. Nightmare Computers. Nightmare Dogs. Junkies. The article is about the advent of cyber-dreams, which are the nightmares of intense computer users. In other words, they can't turn off their computers when they go to sleep. They keep playing "Doom" or crunching data. They don't get much sleep. The sleep-deprived junkies return to their consoles for another fix, each time more depleted and hungrier. The computer dog has eaten, in order, their time, their social lives, their brains, their sleep, and their flesh. They used to have fingers to feel with but they traded them for "digits" in order to perform "digital tasks." They used to have noses, ears, and eyes, but all these

organs have now melted into a single aperture for breathing in the ef-
fluences of the console. As their flesh atrophies, the bytes take over.
These poor rewired wretches crouch in their cubicles absorbed in imaginary communities, filled with fake experiences, surfeited with faux
senses, brimming with phony communication.

The good thing about it, from my point of view, is that the cyber-sphere
doesn't take much room on the real planet, leaving most of it to the rest
of us. In the not very distant future, the cyberspace will in fact detach
itself entirely from this planet and inhabit wholly the ghoulish dimension. I believe that the reason for this migration of people into cyberspace is the fact that not enough people die anymore. The planet is
forcing a solution to overpopulation by disappearing the affluent citizens of the world into the pixel zone. The poor will, of course, continue
to disappear the old-fashioned way, by dying, but there is, you must
admit, some justice in this thinning of the affluent by their own toys.
Computer dog byte nightmare junkie. Hello, Central. Anybody there?

Adding **Memory**

The other day, a friend of mine was explaining how she had to move these pixels around her computer and had to add twenty megabytes of memory to handle the operation. I had the disquieting thought that all this memory she was adding had to come from somewhere. Maybe it was coming from me, because I couldn't remember a thing that day.

And then it became blindingly obvious: *all* the memory that everybody keeps adding to their computers comes from people. Nobody can remember a damn thing. Every time somebody adds some memory to their machine thousands of people forget everything they knew. Americans are singularly devoid of memory these days. We don't remember where we came from, who raised us, when our wars used to be, what happened last year, last month, or even last week. Schoolchildren remember practically nothing. I take the Greyhound bus every week and I swear half the people on there don't know where they got on or where they are supposed to get off.

The explanation is simple: computer companies are stealing human memory to stuff their hard drives. Greyhound, I believe, has some kind of contract with IBM, to steal the memory of everyone riding the bus. They are probably connected by a cable or something: every hundred miles, *poof,* another five hundred megabytes get sucked out of the passengers' brains. The computers' thirst for memory is bottomless: the more they suck the more they need.

Eventually, we will all be walking around with a glazed look in our eyes, trying to figure out who it is we live with. Then we'll forget our names and addresses and we'll just be milling around trying to remember them. The only thing visible about us will be these cables sticking out of our behinds, feeding the scraps of our memory to Computer Central somewhere in Oblivion, U.S.A. I think it's time for all these memory-sucking companies to start some kind of system to feed and shelter us when we forget how to eat, walk, and sleep.

Intelligent
Electronics

I have gone through the hell of trying to figure out my tenth computer in fifteen years and I am just as baffled and irritated as I'd been that fateful day in 1979 when a KayPro4 landed on my desk in Baltimore and screwed up my life forever.

Most of us—techno-idiots who are swept away by superior sales techniques—find ourselves kind of weary, worn out by the losing battle against ever-newer technology. Each new machine humiliates us with identical problems. In the end, we become a little ashamed of confessing our frustrations because it seems that we should have learned something from the last disaster. The stark truth, however, is that no one ever learns anything: he only pretends that he knows something so he won't look the fool. Fools are encouraged by computer PR to think that they know a lot more than they do through the means of so-called user-friendly technologies. There is no such thing: "user-friendly" simply means that our ignorance is now shielded from itself by a screen of faux simplicity that makes it even more difficult to admit our ignorance. Implicitly, both the Macintosh and the Windows programs ask only one question: How can you be so stupid when it's so easy?

Sure. Only I started backwards. From the seeming difficulty of a language called CPM on my KayPro—which looked like a military bunker machine able to take a direct hit from a ten-ton bomb—to the cute faces on my Mac, stretches the vast bridge of fifteen years. For me, these fifteen years represent a certain regression from a poet without any worry or money to the present-day processor of words for articles, radio commentaries, and fiction, and still no money. When I was a young poet in San Francisco in the early seventies, all I needed to practice my profession was a pencil and a bar napkin and the presence of beautiful girls in the vicinity for inspiration. Back then, the streets were full of people who actually lived on them. People used to go to coffeehouses, hang out on their stoops and porches, and gather in large groups to throw Molotov cocktails at the National Guard. I used to write divinely inspired poetry with my pencil on my napkin. I would then read this napkin to a beautiful girl and if she liked it, I would be so inspired I would write another poem on the spot, and if she took me home with her, I would usually write two. Sometimes, I was so poor that I didn't even have a pencil and I used to drink in places where they didn't give you a napkin. On those occasions, my only writing tools might consist of a razor blade and my wrist. With these poetry tools I would then write on the wall—until either a beautiful girl rescued me or the management called an ambulance. That's why I had gotten on to this art in the first place: it was cheap. I didn't need paints and brushes like the painters, or fiddles like the fiddle players, or rich patrons like the sculptors and architects.

Alas. Heaven didn't last long. Enter my first typewriter, a gun blue Smith-Corona 220, ready to fire. Sure enough, I started writing prose: stories, novels, essays. I could only write poetry when I ran out the back door to my bars and cafés. It wasn't easy either: the Smith-Corona was the first of my machines endowed with the ability to hear me leave the house. Often, when I came back late, or left it unattended for a couple of days, the machine would take its revenge on me by smudging or locking or popping a spring.

The KayPro4 marked yet another stage of my enslavement: I have now forgotten just how many months of pain it took finally to produce a printed text through the bowels of it. This "forgetting," by the way, is the computer industry's most precious marketing tool. It is similar to the way women forget the pain of childbirth and go right ahead and have another child. Likewise, we forget the pain of our latest computer: we go right on and get another one. Anyway, the KayPro greatly increased my productivity and severely limited my freedom. Now, this was a paradox because in order to create I needed freedom, but in order to get freedom I had to be away from this machine. It therefore followed that the increased production I obtained from my computer was at the expense of creativity. So I started writing even less poetry.

Don't fear. I will not take you painfully, though it would give me great pleasure, through each and every one of the machines that over the years rapidly turned me into its slave. Suffice it to say that my art became a lot less portable, and even though I have a Mac Notebook now, I find myself bound by habit to the desktop. Once you turn this thing on it starts to blink like a vampire, demanding its quota of words.

Americans have been conquered by the computer. I say conquered to mean what until recently was being called a revolution, the computer revolution. In my opinion it's no longer a revolution: the "compu-revolutionists" have won and there is a New Order in effect. We live in ECC, Era of the Computer Chip, and this technology calls the shots now.

In the previous age, the Early Post-Humanist Age, the issues were about liberation from oppression, freedom from work, spiritual development, the defense of nature, and art. This EPHA (Early Post-Humanist Age) wasn't very long ago; doubtless most of us remember it. Some of us may even believe that we are still in it. Dealing with intelligent electronics does not preclude having a social conscience, it could be argued. Maybe not. But let's see.

The first use of computers for the purpose of social betterment was in the ideologically neutral area of *networking*. It would seem that the increased ability to communicate and to link people of like minds would be a great benefit to people working for post-humanist causes. All the people who want to save the whales could get to know each other and they could link up with the defenders of the wolves and so on. But the actual benefits of networking are not in areas of social activism: they are in fund-raising and marketing. People who might have found solace in the disinterested company of fellow altruists find themselves *targeted* instead. The most vulnerable targets are precisely people who don't cover their asses all the time. The best targets for sales and partisan political rhetoric are people whose minds are still open: but instead of opening them to the common good, the savvy networkers open them to the fangs of the commercial vampire. The proof of this is the tremendous rise of shopping channels, soon to come to your beloved Net, and the Republican sales pitches that translated so well in recent elections.

I know the counterargument: there are efforts to keep the big Net commercial-free but that's like saying, "The Visigoths are still five miles from Rome." And, of course, there are more ways to skin a cat than deafening it with a jingle. From what I've seen, most of the stuff out there is either sex or ads or both. And it's all lies in any case. But let's take the case of a friend of mine in New York who started a special talk salon for high IQs in the hope that world problems would get some armchair brainstorms. Guess what? The high IQs, after some high-minded protocol dust, got right down to business: sex and money. If they had been meeting face to face, I doubt that they had been this crass. Face to face one tries to find one's better nature. If only because one has some vestigial respect, or fear, of the other's soul. In the anonymity of the electronic exchange one finds the crassest thing first. The soul doesn't shine through. Intelligence does, yes, but intelligence without soul is like a fiddle without strings.

Okay, I'm no prude, and I'm not blind to the practical advantages of information in medicine and other industries. It's the creativity angle I'm working. To be creative, a person needs freedom. I've said that before, but let me ask you: is freedom increased or lessened by the use of a computer? I would say lessened if not entirely eliminated. First, you are bound to the keyboard. Second, you must respond to the time-consuming demands of (mostly) useless information. Third, you do not have the luxury of being able to reflect for long periods of time because, most likely, the clock is ticking. Fourth, you are connected willy-nilly to a community of users with whom you have nothing in common but the frustrations of the equipment. Time is a limited commodity, which has become ever more limited since the Industrial Revolution. With the latest computer technology, human time disappears completely: machine time takes over.

Okay, you might say, but this "time," this "freedom" that you say we used to have—it was time for what? Freedom to do what? Here we come to the crux of the problem. The question of information.

ECC (Era of the Computer Chip) is also called, sometimes, the Age of Information. It's not a bad name: it describes succinctly exactly what it is that we produce and consume now. An observer in, let's say, the sixteenth century would be astonished to see the quantities of sheer information consumed by an average American in an average town on an average day. Our sixteenth-century observer would, at first, faint from the sheer excitement and delight at the volume of knowledge, and then would try to grab as much of it as possible. He or she would, however, be able to grab no more than about five minutes' worth from our media before short-circuiting and vanishing in a puff of smoke. Why would a sixteenth-century observer short-circuit? Because a sixteenth-century observer, unlike a twentieth-century consumer, would try to make sense of the information by connecting it. A sixteenth-century human was probably the last being on the planet capable of knowing everything—and not just *knowing,* but having a connected picture of the universe in his or her head.

To be sure, this was a sixteenth-century European, and the *everything* he or she knew was only what had been written and translated in Europe. Still, that was a lot, considering that knowing so much involved making a great many connections in order to make sense of the information. After the Renaissance, the illusion of such knowing vanished: libraries became the repositories of all that humanity knew. It no longer became necessary to know everything: little by little people began to specialize in small areas, trusting that they could find what they needed by looking it up. Instead of a coherent picture of the world that each individual might, by reflection, form for oneself, we entered an age of fragmentation. In this age, no individual had more than a few pieces of the puzzle and they lay disconnected, waiting for this individual to connect them with information from the library. Information increased and libraries grew and grew until there was a problem of storage. Happily, computers showed up.

Now the problem of storage seems to have been solved, leaving only—only!—the problem of meaning. This, of course, is not such a great problem: very intelligent computers, very fast ones, could supply information almost as quickly as one's own memory used to when one had a memory. Fast computers are, in effect, a still-clumsy global nervous system that will get less and less clumsy.

So, what's the problem? The problem is that the storage space now far exceeds the amount of information we have to store in it. Everything we know can now be stored in a corner of the vast electronic storage bin. The storage space now begins to demand information from us at a faster and faster rate: in order to fill its insatiable and theoretically infinite maw we must now produce faster and faster and more and more.

Very soon, like that Renaissance person, we will blow up and go up in smoke, not because we have too much in us to deal with, but because we don't have another thing to give to the machine that's sucked us dry.

When the Renaissance persons put what they knew in books and put these in libraries, they didn't have to hurry. They emptied themselves of the information that held their world together slowly because there was only so much room. We now have to empty ourselves fast of information that literally goes through us. We have no time to reflect on it, we have no time to construct a picture of the world for ourselves. We are simply extensions of the intelligent electronics demanding to be fed.

When I hear "virtual world" or "cyberspace" I think of archeology. I *already* think of this world space as an archeological site, our equivalent of the Roman temple. At this point in time, and maybe for another decade, the temple of virtuality is awake with the swoosh of information it sucks to feed itself. In a decade or so the info will be exhausted. There will be nothing to suck and the whoosh will die down. Already, all the inert info we've busy-stashed like squirrels in books, tapes, and now CD-ROM, has whooshed down the cyber-gullet. The cyber-temple walls are so vast that all our records take only a pinprick's worth of room. So, what happens when the info's been all stored and all the things you can do to move it up and down and sideways have taken their thimble's worth of space? Well, then, what happens is that the temple itself, deprived of its food, will start to eat at its own walls until they collapse on top of everyone in it—and everyone *is* or will be shortly within—and that will be the end of our particular world and culture. Thus, archeology. They'll dig up cyberspace like Apulum and they'll say: They worshipped their gods in here and when they ran out of sacrifices their gods killed them.

The meaning of virtuality is the information used in constructing it. Virtuality only has meaning as long as it's under construction. Nobody can actually inhabit it: it has no smell. Or, as my friend Larry says: "You can't pass a joint through the Internet!" Once virtuality has been built out of all the information we have, it becomes meaningless. And we are empty, emptied by what we have given virtuality. This is the case of any temple: it has meaning only as long as it has belief. When belief is exhausted it collapses. Information in our age is a dangerous belief: we worship information. We believe in storing it and, in so doing, we are drafted to serve the architecture of the store. The original purpose of information was to mobilize the interior of the mind for deeper understanding. In order to be useful in that way it had to stay within. By giving it up to the computer, we have not only precluded our evolution but have insured our obsolescence.

Okay, so I'm no Marshall McLuhan, who thought that the global village was just hunky-dory. But I'm no practicing Luddite, either. I'm writing this on my latest tormentor, a Packard-Bell 486, courtesy of my mother, who always had a knack for interrupting whatever I was doing. This particular interruption took a week. Mothers are probably in collusion with intelligent electronics—to keep everybody in where they can keep an eye on them. But mother is too big a subject, let me go back to the questions of freedom and time, "down time" as it is now called.

Yes, freedom, and time, and the question of what does a "coherent picture of the world" mean. Freedom is that referent-free space at the coffeehouse when you scribble on your napkin with the vague perfume of that potential girl in your unfocused nostrils. In that state, time is infinite. Not machine time, not clock time, not set-up time: infinity. (And that's not a car, please!) In this space of infinity-freedom you dream. You float, you dream, you have no boundaries, you are within a potential and generative state of mind. This is the mulch ground of the uncreated, the space prior to inarticulation, a place where articulation is, in fact, suspect. You are . . . in New Orleans.

You look out the frame of the streetcar window and let the live oaks and the big houses with their columns of piquant stories flash by without focusing on any of them. You go to Cafe Brazil and inhale deeply the aroma of espresso and young dancers at work. You go to the Faulkner Bookstore and say hi to his ghost. You hand over some money to the tap dancers on Decatur Street. Get immersed in street music. And this is no interactive program: things smell, resonate, and brace.

Under conditions of freedom and leisure, an individual might construct a picture of the world from the few bits of information still charged by the senses. It won't be the Renaissance cat's erudite, prescientific vision, but it won't be the overnetworked grudge's sense of eternal emergency, either.

Some **Remarks** on **Interactivity** (With a **Little** Treatise on Language)

After two days of listening to talk about the new media I feel like the old Jew in the Soviet Union who wanted to emigrate just before the collapse of Communism. He asked the border guard for a globe to see where he should go. After studying it, he returned it and asked: Do you have another globe?

Nothing I have yet heard has convinced me that the utopian globe being dangled before us by compucrats has any livable place on it. There is even a question as to whether it exists. Like God and utopia it depends largely on the amount of faith you bring to it. Cyberspace may turn out to be another utopia like the one the old Jew was trying to leave behind. Communism was a virtual world that existed only in the heads of people who ran the state and the police who made sure that people kept the faith. What if cyberspace turns out to be just a holding tank for a new mass of believers? Believers who *think* that they are part of a community, who *think* that they are sincere ("best thought, first thought," said Allen Ginsberg) but, in effect, are just extorted of time, energy, and body by an imaginary space owned by alien military forces (i.e., ours)?

Call it oversensitivity to utopian disappointments, but a modicum of philosophical paranoia is in order. Is the new interactivity a clever TV door opening into another TV, a big telephone with pictures and sounds? Or is it a whole new rewiring of what little remains of sense-impoverished humans?

Of the more meaningless jargon words I repeatedly hear is the one called "content." I heard grown-ups cry for "content" the way believers cry for a deliverer, a Messiah. We have the forms, oh Heavenly Chip, now send us The Content! Well, it won't happen, no matter how much conceptual sweat goes into "content betterment" because form never precedes content. Form is always an extension of content. Shakespeare didn't invent drama and then pour some content into it. *Everything* is content, we are drowning in it, *there is nothing but content.* The only trouble is that it's just raw matter, not art. Art is what is really being called for.

Allow me to experiment with a random construction. For about two weeks I kept track of mentions of computers and attendant phenomena in newspapers and sometimes on the radio. I didn't search these out. These are merely the casual, coincidental items that pass through the attention field of an average newspaper reader and less-than-average TV watcher. I'm sure that if I'd paid attention I would have found more.

On May 23, 1995, "Dear Abby" answered a plea for help from a woman whose mate was obsessed with the computer.

> *Dear Abby,*
> *My husband is a junkie, and it's ruining our marriage. Sometimes he spends as much as ten hours a day on the computer. He has gone on from being a handsome, outgoing, affectionate husband to an overweight, un-caring, temperamental roommate. Is there a support group for wives like me?*
>
> *Computer-Widow*

To which Abby responds, typically, but also unusually: "A counselor can help him face the 'demon.'"

The counselor bit is typical, but the business about the "demon" is not. Abby is expressing a widely held but underreported belief that the computer is the Devil. Television is believed by some religious sects to be the Devil, or at least his mouthpiece, and I'm not sure that I disagree. And if the TV is the Devil, the computer is the Devil squared because its interactivity allows for clearing away whatever objections one might have for being tied to one's chair and wired directly into the Mass Brain. Look at it from the Computer-Widow's point of view: the fingers of the man who used to touch her have now become digits good only for the keyboard. His eyes, which used to look at her, are now following little spurts of light on a screen. His feet, which used to move, are now useless. Let's face it, this man no longer has a body and he has lost all his senses except one: the eyeball that tracks the track ball. He has all but disappeared.

The Computer-Widow is too distraught to ask where he's disappeared to. He's in hyperspace, but she doesn't want to go there after him because then she too would lose her body and her senses. Like Orpheus descending into Hell, she'd need a lot of help. Abby's typical answer will not suffice: there are no counselors for this kind of thing. The computer junkie is quite happy: he is with his own, at the Cyber-Bar in Hell, singing interactive songs until they pull his credit. Then even his cyberspace nonexistence will cease. Banished from Hell. Oh, horror!

We move on to Thursday, May 25, 1995, when we hear about "Love at First Megabyte," from Sherri Winston, in an article subtitled "On-Line Intimacy Has Spread Like a Virus." Notice how clever Sherri—or the headline writer—is: they have gotten a whole lot of interactivity into the mix: a vampire's bite has met the megabyte, human viruses have become linked to computer viruses. The man-machine mix is so smooth you can barely see the wires. And Sherri's cleverness continues paragraph after paragraph, as she describes rooms full of people discussing intimate details, which, as she puts it, "lovers would not ordinarily share." She describes these rooms for "no more than 23 people" as real rooms until she reveals, inevitably, their virtuality. There is something in the cuteness of that predictable revelation that is more than mere bad writing. Sherri shares with us a current commonplace: virtuality is really cute. It's just like reality, only better, because it hurts only virtually. It's also better because it's more naughty. Notice that these love rooms hold "up to 23 people," which is sort of ironic but also titillating because it's an orgy. Sherri wouldn't be caught dead in a real orgy, of course, but a virtual orgy, hey, the sky's the limit, long live the imagination!

I will refrain from quoting the extraordinary inanities that pour out of these people and their so-called on-line counselors. It is as if these people, who had been dumb, mute, and inarticulate until now, had been given suddenly the gift of speech and are now handing their inner souls over for inspection to twenty-three others. What a miracle! A virtual miracle anyway. The truth is that these people are not really speaking, but lying. Even if they are not consciously lying, which they probably are, they are doing so because the paucity of their vocabulary is matched only by the underdeveloped state of their psyches.

It would be interesting to compare the Net with familiar versions of the afterlife. Is it hell or is it heaven? What they *do* have in common is a suspension of time. If you're dead it doesn't much matter, but if you're alive this suspension is actually theft. Your time isn't being suspended, it's stolen. Are we witnessing a massive extortion of time? The Computer-Widow was a modern version of the Talmud widow. The study of the Torah absorbed all of the Talmudist's time. All he did was study, study, study the little windows in the Bible that led to other, equally opaque windows. The Talmudist was well respected because his continual study insured an afterlife for the whole family. But now that the whole family is flying from window to window the afterlife is here. In the future, who'll do the cooking and the washing?

Thank God for the Third World.

On May 22, 1995, the *New York Times,* under the heading "Digital Commerce," broke the bad news that "Innovation appears to be a scarce commodity. How will multimedia's new talent emerge from the interactive ooze?"

I sort of like the idea here that talent like life is born out of ooze, but also the assumption that new talent for the intermedia must, of necessity, come from the ooze of the multimedia itself. This is absolutely accurate and it answers its own question: the talent that is lacking is lacking because it hasn't yet been born. The multimedia users who speak its idiom are still too young to have left the ooze to innovate. One could say the same thing about the audience. The *New York Times* goes on to scoff at the current glut of CD-ROMs as "multimillions of dollars spent on mediocrity." This is doubtlessly true, but why should the multimedia be any different from the "uni-media," which, right now, spends *billions* on mediocrity? If the interactive idiom is indeed just an idiom, you can be mediocre in it just as you can be mediocre in English. But if the interactive idiom is not just an idiom but several, a kind of multi-idiom, than you can be a multi-idiot, which is a new thing indeed.

Television has already replaced the hierarchical book with the simultaneous image, short-circuiting in the process all ability to respond critically. The untended senses may, however, grow monstrous in the dark, so multimedia can now satisfy these atrophied senses by giving them their own kind of TV. This is one more way to reinvent the wheel, virtually: by appealing to several senses at once (ear, eye, nose, and, hopefully, throat), multi-idiocy can bypass *all* critical senses.

It is hard, since Marshall McLuhan, not to fetishize the new media as the latest revolution in outlook. Are we being completely rewired, once more, or is this just another way to extort our human energies in order to make a huge, heartless machine run? One thing is clear: McLuhan's global village is a nasty place. The villagers are in a bad mood and you can't eat virtual potatoes.

The May/Summer 1995 issue of the *AWP Chronicle*, a writers' trade journal, has an article called "Myth and the Internet Community," subheaded "Disappearing Authors & Disappearing Readers." The author, W. Scott Olsen, starts by praising what he calls his "mythic community," fellow writers around the country and the globe, engaged in a fluid conversation about writing. He quotes a warning from the opening screen of something called WriteMUSH: "Something to remember: this is a game. People play characters. You have no way of knowing what they are like outside of this game except what they choose to tell you. Caveat Emptor." Mr. Olsen comments then that "the mythic community is becoming a type of replacement for the real community."

Herein lies an interesting thought. The thrust of good art, I believe, has always been to reveal something of the truth of human beings, to reveal, that is, precisely the thing or things that lie beyond the web of deceptions and virtualities that everybody weaves about themselves. One of the major questions of literature always had to do with the tension between the persona and the private (or real) person. Literature explores this problem via society and its pressure on individuals to be something other than they are. The Web (apt name) encourages the fabrication of personae. It is thus an effort contrary to art the way we have known it. It encourages the fabrication of masks while it makes it impossible to know anything other than the representation. You can say that it is better suited to blackmail and cons than to revelation. On the other hand, you can say the same thing about any writing or speech that isn't art. The question then for the working artist is: What are the best ways to explore the space between the mask and the person in the interactive idiom? Is it, in fact, possible? Or is the medium fundamentally postmodern in the sense that, like an onion, there are only layers, no truth?

Mr. Olsen also bemoans briefly the problem of the lack of editing on the Net and quotes an article by Christine Nystrom on "The Crisis of Narrative":

> Biology provides every creature and species with "filters" for sensory data, thresholds and barriers to sensation and perception, structures that direct and limit what can be seen, felt, heard, and attended to. Without such structures, which function as biological commands to "Ignore function," sensory creatures would be inundated by detail and difference, overwhelmed by choice, paralyzed by change.

"In the literary world," comments Mr. Olsen, "editors and readers can act as this selective and affirming filter. In the virtual world, such filters are mostly absent."

To this, I can only refer back to Dante's circle number four in Hell, which is also the place where the Computer-Widow's husband went. It's a world where everyone babbles, lies, preens, begs, and extorts. The repressed, the buried, the unconscious, the debris, the flotsam, the snot, the unplugged toilet that is humanity in the dark, expand like a black hole. This may not be the Net you all know and love, but then people are still pretty inarticulate. Wait until they discover the *redemptory* quality of the virtual world. When they discover that virtuality is a form of immortality. Then, in addition to being whatever it is now, the Net will become a safety deposit box for the thoughts of dying people. In other words, we will all become the repositories of strangers' *timor mortis*.

Dear Miss Manners,
A man who said he was about to die has chosen me and twenty-two other people in Love Abattoir No. 29 to confess to a heinous crime. He cooked his wife and children and served them file'd on a bed of greens with a light pesto sauce at his church picnic yesterday. What should I do? Call the authorities? Twenty-one of my twenty-two fellow abattorians are of the opin-

*ion that No. 29 is as sacred as a priest's confessional and that we are bound
by room solidarity to support rather than destroy our brother. Is it okay to
disagree? What do you think? What should I do?*

Troubled in the Abattoir.

Dear Troubled:
   *Twenty-two people can be wrong. I would advise you to follow your con-
science. But ask yourself some hard questions first. Who were his wife and
children? You didn't know them? Perhaps they deserved to be cooked.*

Sorry. I'm a fiction writer, too. Miss Manners never had to answer this
question but Miss Manners *did* proffer an opinion on Net manners on
Sunday, May 28, 1995. She praised the ethics of cyberspacers under
the head, "Young cybercitizens discover etiquette need." "Today's young
adults," she tells us, "rediscovered the value of etiquette when they
started forming a new type of community—the Internet."

Miss Manners believes, as many of us do, in the inherent goodness
of youth. Children are naturally gracious, they have an innate sense of
right and wrong. She may be right. I believe in the superiority of childhood. But children don't dominate or own the Net: adults do. Young
adults. Young adults may still have some of the good sense of children
but, for the most part, they are predators.

In cyberspace, Miss Manners really ought to be God, or at least Tsar,
given ultimate power of banishment. It's an expanding universe and it
needs a thundering etiquette boss.

Why agonize over the moral quality of the virtual? In the real world you
have your hellish slums of Calcutta and you have Place Clichy in Paris.
Why not have your perfectly civilized virtual place where everyone is
clean, sexy, and musical? And those who like nasty stuff, can always
go to Marseilles. Well, yes, but the key word to remember here is *virtual*. It's not real: clean, sexy, and musical could be dirty, gross, and dis-
sonant. There is no art by which to know any differently: virtually, any
stink can become perfume.

Which is fine, once again, if you thrive in postmodernity.

On May 28, 1995, James Mayer of Newhouse News service writes,
under the heading "Cyberspace cultural clash spawns ethical bound-

aries," that millions of settlers are coming to the Internet, bringing with them a clash of cultures. The questions raised are, he says:

> Should sexually explicit material, hate speech, or other potentially of-fensive stuff such as bomb recipes be controlled or is control possible in an electronic world with no boundaries and no central authority?
>
> How can we protect our privacy in a rapidly expanding information universe?
>
> How do we balance anonymity and responsibility in a world where people can go anywhere, be anybody, and say anything?
>
> Can cyberspace survive commerce? Can it survive without it? How long will there be before there is a billboard every few yards on the in-formation superhighway?

Mr. Mayer then reviews a number of proposals before Congress dealing with these issues, and concludes that in cyberspace "there's always an-other frontier, because it expands with the population. It's not so much the final frontier as it is the endless frontier."

Mr. Mayer's metaphors interest me because they come from my neigh-borhood. Immigration, the frontier, expanding borders, limits, and the legislation of these things, is an area of great interest to me in the real world because I'm an immigrant, a border crosser, a partisan of liberty and freedom of movement, and a traveler. But what do these things mean in the virtual world?

I became quite suspicious of the use of such metaphors when I heard that Newt Gingrich supports the wide use of computers. He would even offer a tax credit to ousted welfare recipients so that they can buy a computer and stay home. Instead of digging the streets, I suppose. In practical terms, his Contract with America is really a Contract with the Suburbs. Ideally, right-wing, Republican America would be a series of small communities linked by computers. The cities are conspicuously missing from this map. I have always suspected that at heart this coun-try's right-wingers would like to throw a ring of fire around the cities, and would help them to self-destruct because, after all, their enemies are all in the cities: liberals, Jews, Negroes, immigrants. How much bet-ter if the actual cultural laboratories of the cities could be replaced by the babble of virtual communities exchanging Christmas greetings and stock tips. The real American century would thus be replaced by the virtual American century, a bloodless and gutless place where even wars can be fought from a distance on your home computer, without once see-

ing the faces of your victims, but seeing, rather, the happy faces of
Techne, the always-smiling Virtuality.

A Little Treatise on Language

Don't get me wrong: I can make speech with the best of them. Language is something people ask me to use in exchange for money so I do
it. Occasionally, I even use language for the sheer pleasure of hearing
it sound and rebound in the ear of fellow creature. The pleasure that is
returned by creature is payment too, for using language well. One thing
we know about language is that its skillful use is rewarding. Speaking
several of them is severally rewarding. Because of this, humans continually improve their languages, invent twists on their sounds, fill old
noises with new meaning, and, generally, dress their emotional repertoire in language as soldiers dress for parades.

That said, it would be a great mistake to believe, as many people do,
that language communicates the truth of one's human condition or even
the truth of one's observations. The communicative abilities of language, despite the fact that that's what we *seem* to be using it for, are severely restricted. Language can make things happen: you can start a riot,
make someone write you a check, or deceive your mother, but language
comes no closer to the truth than crying or picking your nose will. The
truth is that language is a virtual means of communication and, like anything virtual, it is limitless in its ability to imitate anything, including
sincerity. The key to language and to virtuality is imagination. You can
be fat and scrofulous in reality, but in language and virtuality you are
Nastassia Kinski in *Tess* by Roman Polanski.

(The only approaches to truth by means of language are artistic. Art
is what walks the narrows because art is capable of supporting paradoxes. It is also capable of constructing myths and stories that are little engines of reflection.)

Because of its proven record in improving one's chances for survival
and satisfaction, language has become a metaphor for a great many
things that fall outside its purview. It is said, for instance, that there is
a "gestural language," meaning all the signals we send out with our bodies. There are "animal languages," as well as "the language of nature,"
by which is meant, I believe, the ability to recognize patterning and to
call it whatever you want. These language metaphors are not the same
as idioms. Idioms, I believe, are language-derived or language-organized
systems that function exactly like language with the important differ-

ence that they are private property while language qua language belongs to everybody.

An idiom is language owned by a profession, field, or subculture. What you are calling here "the interactive idiom" is a gang jargon that has gone haywire, and is threatening to become a kind of esperanto. Esperanto, you may recall, was a synthetic mishmash constructed by some utopia-struck enthusiasts who believed that a universal language spoken rationally by reasonable people might check our tendency to murder each other. They believed that if the inexplicable inability to understand each other precisely were to be expunged we might live in our world as sanely as German housewives appear to live in their kitchens. I'm not being flip here: take the difference between a German kitchen, *Küche* of the 1930s, and an automated American kitchen of the 1960s. The same word denotes both, but the difference isn't merely temporal or spacial. In the 1930s, the German *Küche* was part of the national-socialist ideal for German women of *"Kirche, Küche, Kinder,"* (church, kitchen, children) while the American automatic kitchen of the 1960s was the opposite, embodying the ideal of the liberated woman in the age of contraceptives, self-medication, and the job market. Now if German and American kitchens fairly close in time can exemplify such distinctions, imagine an eleventh-century Chinese kitchen, or the field kitchen of Gilles de Rais, Jeanne d'Arc's monstrous lieutenant. You probably can't, not right at this moment, anyway, but this is only a small example of the physical, affective universe that surrounds words in every language. The English or American "home" is not the French *"chez moi."* There is history, spatial context, memory, smell, and touch that are automatically contained in the word. It's a credit to tolerance that the proponents of esperanto weren't strung up when they showed up with that mutated horror, that simplified interactivity.

The last attempt to build a universal translator was the utopia of state Communism. So-called reason, scientific objectivity, the laws of history, and dialectical materialism were used as conceptual blocks to create a universal idiom. It is clear now that what shipwrecked the utopia was the stubborn persistence of ethnic differences, which, being suppressed, turned malignant.

Two quick thoughts then, given the complexity of the world versus the paucity of idiom: The first is that *words are merely words.* They are unsteady signs pointing to what they cannot express. To quote an old poem: "All sound is religion. Language is merely a choirboy in this religion." The second is that the so-called interactive idiom will either go wild and become a generalized cacophony or it will be harnessed, given a grammar, and set to work for Microsoft. In either case, it is interesting to watch, if you don't get too close. (Speaking for myself, of course.)

In the nineteenth century in Romania two schools fought for control of the language: the Latinists and the Slavophiles. Their clashes were not just over grammar and vocabulary but also over the soul of the nation. The psychic shape of the future nation rode on the decision. In the end, neither school won out because the living speakers of the language determined their own direction, which reflected their reality. But the learned schools had one thing in common, despite their differences: they insisted on banishing from the language foreign expressions, border slang, Gypsy jive. While most academies have now given up trying to purify the language, the French have not. The Academie Française still bans and even "executes" words, particularly American ones, which they perceive, quite rightly, to be carriers of cultural viruses.

The so-called interactive idiom has all sorts of pitfalls ahead of it: 1, esperantoism, with its attendant suppression of differences and oversimplification; 2, exclusivism, which is a copyrighted grammar; 3, limitlessness.

I already mentioned esperantoism and I touched a bit on exclusivism. The third pitfall, limitlessness, is more serious. Human idiom is limited while machine idiom is *unlimited.* The interactive idiom may turn out to be a one-way conversation: the tireless machine will keep talking while the exhausted human will fall silent. We may really be talking about the *active idiom* of the machine versus the silence of the human. The ability of the machine to reproduce ad infinitum is certain to suppress any other idiom, particularly human ones, and to produce infinite and passive esperanto.

Which is why it is important, I believe, to return to the actual position and dimensions of language in a universe that is alive, mysterious, and much vaster than the noises we make toward each other. It is necessary to keep languages, idioms, and communication in perspective. They are fragile constructs hedged in by vast areas of what is unexpressed, unarticulated, and undiscovered. At the same time, we are also operating in a vast garbage dump of everything that we humans have rejected since we began. In other words, things that *have* been expressed, articulated, and *discarded.* This stuff is a kind of unconscious that is resurfacing, I'm afraid, on the Internet. A lot of what I personally hoped never to have to deal with again is showing up like space garbage on my screen. Every bad version of every bad thought I ever had is out there being taught by somebody and posted. My friend Ted Thomas called this a kind of "electronic Epsom salts" that draws out the black humors. On the other hand, the return of the repressed may in itself be liberating. Much of what has been repressed has been thrown out by edict by those in power. It is possible also that a kind of healing lies in watching the ghosts of our private and collective past come back to life. I kind of doubt it, but the question is worth asking: Is interactivity, in the process of becoming language, pulling up much of what has been repressed and forgotten? And if so, what does it do to those who thought they were moving ahead, into uncharted territory?

Just Another Cyber-Day

In a recent issue of *Wired* I found two items of interest. The first was a full-page picture of my former student and friend, Robert Toups, all naked, except for a Mac laptop in front of his um . . . front. He was thus displayed because he has become an overnight success in cyberspace owing to his "Babes-on-the-Web" web site. Apparently, he rates photos of women on the Internet and thus provides a valuable service for those who don't have the time to cruise on their own. I didn't teach him any of this when he was in my class. He learned all this on his own, like the good Bush-era college kid he was, one who naturally likes Rush Limbaugh and thinks that Newt Gingrich is the Messiah.

The second item, in the same issue of *Wired* was an interview with the Messiah himself. Newt Gingrich is a big fan of the Internet and a computer prophet. His famous remark about outfitting ghetto dwellers with laptops was controversial but catchy. The only trouble with it is that he'd cut off milk and bread in exchange. We all know how tasty plastic is. That aside, the Speaker's replies to the *Wired* questions were interesting because he does indeed think that he's the Messiah. He accepts the epithet "visionary" and is quite at ease with his duty to save the world. To accomplish this, he says, "We have to do nine things in parallel," and then proceeds to enumerate them. These things sound reasonable but why nine and not ten or five?

I suspect that this is a mind that will not accept chaos, fog, fuzz, paradox, or ambiguity. Unfortunately, the world is all of those and there are lots and lots of real people between those nine points who aren't on-line, but live in throbbing, hungry, messy cities. Are these the people to be saved or eliminated? Is there a world already saved, inhabited by Robert with his laptop and by Newt with his? Are these worlds compatible or even comparable?

Swimming Between Languages

Part 3

Life Against Art

Art is neat, life is messy. Any artist knows that real people are trouble. In some cases, it's good trouble. Ronald Reagan's bad movies became a lot more interesting after Reagan became President. But sometimes it's bad trouble. Professor John Biguenet, who tracks this sort of thing, tells me that biographies are notoriously vulnerable. Their subjects will rise from the dead and kill their biographers. Custer was a good guy for a stretch of books, then up came a new p.o.v. and the chief's in the doghouse now, his partisans dead meat. Some truly ugly subject like Nixon gets tossed around by posterity for a while and comes up prettier than he did at first.

Some artists calculate revision into the product, figuring they'll get there before history messes with it. Andrew Wyeth's model, Helga, after a long and deliberate sojourn in the closet made a multimillion-dollar outing on the covers of news magazines. It was Wyeth's way of saying, Hey, I'm not this sunny New England painter, I have shadows, and I want the money now.

In all these cases, though, trouble doesn't come from the artists' subjects but from time, which has a way of messing with everything including your idea of yourself. Mostly, the victims of art have little to say about it after they've been locked up within the frame of a picture, between the covers of a book, or inside a reel of film.

The French writer Raymond Queneau wrote a book called *The Flight of Icarus* where the characters of some bad French writers escape from their books and go on to live a life different from the one planned for them. But where do they go to live it? In Queneau's book.

I once wrote an autobiography and my mother didn't talk to me for a year. She didn't recognize herself. Recently, I made a movie with some psychics in it and now they don't like how they came out. What kind of psychics are these? Couldn't they tell how they were going to come out?

Let's face it, if you're alive, stay out of art. If you're a nice person with good self-esteem and you see a camera, a pencil, or a paintbrush coming your way, run like hell. It's history coming to mug you.

Paradise

The biblical Garden of Eden always seemed to me an unbelievably boring place, begging for vandalism. Every day the same weather, no sex, no fruit, no thought, no language. Adam sees Eve. Eve sees Adam. Nothing to say. Nothing to do. No hello. No good-bye. Keep circling. God always spying. No wonder they went nuts. Went for the nuts. Blame the nuts.

Now comes *The Lost Book of Paradise,* restored by David Rosenberg from old manuscripts and ancient longings, a poetic rendering of a paradise stormy with emotional deprivation and strife. In Rosenberg's paradise, nature is alive, more alive than Adam who longs for Eve, just like fruits and nuts long for bees and bugs. Adam is alone for a long time, shapeless and without a mirror, until Eve shows up out of his own desire and together they sing to each other until they upset the more practical fruits and flowers, and then God, who likes a balanced and harmonious garden, throws them out.

The Lost Book of Paradise is a whodunit, with David Rosenberg as the detective, tracking down the author through lost cities and libraries of the ancient world. The author of *The Lost Book* is a woman, a scholar from the ninth century before the Christian era, who is herself a detective seeking the lost story of paradise. Paradise itself exists nowhere outside fragments of poetry, shreds of song, interrupted longings. In the end, it's a love story between two poet-scholars: a contemporary one, David Rosenberg, and an ancient one, a woman who sprang from his desire and imagination. It occurred to me, after reading this, that the only paradise there ever was was a love song. The Garden of Eden was a song. Still, the humans did sing louder than all the things of nature, and for that they were punished with silence and deafness and the inability to understand the language of flowers and beasts. As punishment, they write books. And wail for the "lost paradise."

The Lost Book of Paradise, restored by David Rosenberg (New York: Hyperion, 1993). Rosenberg is the coauthor of *The Book of J*, the bible written by a woman.

Sex, the World

The root of the brain wherein Eros dwells is older and deeper than the house of language. When languages, in their youthful diversity, visit the cave of Eros, they shed their differences and take on a respectful universality. Which is not to say that vivid pungencies and distinct vibratory differences do not overcome the reader. They do. Genders are distinct, cultures are particular, the paths to Eros complex. Different languages maintain diverse love poetries, translators add their own musk, but writing issuing from Eros is unmistakably universal. This, in the end, is our delight and reward for having sustained the prolonged reflection occasioned by reading erotica. In other words, sex is itself a language here, a language in which a writer can say anything that matters to him or her, just as he or she would say it in Romanian, Chinese, or French.

In Romania, as in other ex-Red fiefdoms, sex was a form of protest. Our encounters gave the finger to the Communist Party and the puritanical state it had created. Since we couldn't speak, we coupled. But Eros did not necessarily gain thereby. Our couplings were defiant, obscene, guilty, drunken, unsafe. In the last decade of the Ceauşescu dictatorship, Romanian families were required to produce five children apiece. Abortion was illegal, birth control nonexistent. Unwanted children filled orphanages. Many people refused to have sex altogether. The libido of the nation plunged, along with the birthrate.

Ceauşescu's Romania makes a brief appearance in a story called "The Highway," by Iva Pekarkova. A young Czech hitchhiker is perched in the high cabin of a huge truck that passes like an ocean liner through the brine of sorrow and poverty that lines the Romanian roads. The truck driver, Sami, her lover, bestows (for a hefty price) condoms on the starved natives. They trade everything for these precious objects that contain the promise of brief pleasure without dire consequences. Ironically, Sami, the agent of freedom, is a Turk, part of a nation that once oppressed Romanians. He is besieged by young Romanian women for whom the big truck is a possible means of escape. The young Czech hitchhiker is suffused with pathos: her sexual opening to the world corresponds with the darkest hour of Communism in Eastern Europe. She defies the borders of state with her young girl fever. And we know what happened: she won.

What happened *after* she won is told with no less pathos in "Reds," a story by Lila Lahavitsky, in which a young Russian woman laments the abduction of her lover by "a woman with long red hair from the West who comes and steals him." Political freedom has come, but with it has come also the temptation and greed of the outside. This woman, lamenting in mythic tones the absence of her man is no other than Mother Russia herself who, in the depth of her sorrow and in the unstilled ache of her desire, is nostalgic now for the brutal but safe lust of the past.

In both these stories, sex struggles symbolically against the strictures of politics. But this contest between sex and politics is reversed in Ivan Klima's "An Incomprehensible Choice," where, quite the contrary, desire makes politics irrelevant. A young married woman falls in love with an older, crippled neighbor. In addition to his evident drawbacks, this man is also a messy bachelor, and a fascist—an utterly repulsive and, ultimately, weak man. But desire is mysterious and the young heroine, alone and helpless at the end, understands even less than we do what has so devastated and swept her away. Which is not to say that Ivan Klima's story is not political: the politics is not of the moment, though. Old histories, barely comprehensible, speak through us and vibrate in our cells. In the encounters of people, whole ancestral crowds stand in expectant anticipation behind and above, filled with bright hope, their ghostly nostrils flaring with lust.

From politics to history, the road, in Ludvik Vaculik's "The Herb of Forgetting," leads through the maze of desire itself, made complicated by religion and psychology. We are still in Eastern Europe, in Prague. Our protagonists are churchgoing Catholics in post-Communism, which is to say neo-post-Catholics. They go to Mass, but they have read Nietzsche and they have sex. In order to come together, they must first recapitulate, like phylogeny, the origins and history of love, which they do, by retranslating the classic torments of love into their own givens. In the end, these two did not have to be Czech at all: they have broken out into modernity, into the West.

Some erotic stories by Latin Americans and Chinese writers mirror the beginnings and the middles of the idealism from which the Eastern Europeans have just escaped. Claribel Alegria's story "Paradise" is set in a postrevolutionary Nicaragua at the very moment that disillusionment sets in. The heroine is waiting in her car outside a motel room where she has taken her younger friend, who is a virgin, and one of her older lovers, who is going to relieve the girl of her embarrassment. The woman in the car believes that she is doing her innocent friend a favor, but the longer she waits the more tawdry the situation appears, particularly in light of her own disappointments, both sexual and political. One can taste, in this story, the bitter but still fresh roots of political idealism: the heroine's disappointment is kin to Mayakovsky's after the Russian revolution.

It is much later in the revolution for the heroes of Ha Jin's "Broken." This is the time in China of the Revolutionary Guards during the Cultural Revolution. This attempt to revive enthusiasm for old man Mao's youth is doomed by the conformism already bred into the young Chinese. The only energy they bring to their revolution is brutality. A young girl is framed and punished for her sexuality which, even in its debased and humiliated form, serves to titillate the repressed revolutionaries.

The young man who is forced to collaborate with the brutal guards is a conformist who wishes only to get ahead. To this end he is advised to "improve his writing," which is a sure path to advancement. As it turns out, there is a lot more to advancement than calligraphy, yet the "writing" remains ominously present. The corrupt world of the Chinese revolutionary guards is held together by writing: confessions, denunciations, reports, memos. This is, make no mistake, Mandarin China. The opposite of writing is sex. But even writing about sex is bound by rules about writing.

The West is where all that is written about sex resides. Europe and America are the libraries and laboratories of sexual analysis, interpretation, and dissemination. But beyond that, Western democracies are also the source of feminist and gender revolutions. Democracies are exporters of the erotic, from feminist revolution to pornography. They are also importers. From here in the West we can proceed in any direction: geographically around the globe, or vertically into the past or the future. All this seismic wealth is, however, the source of an unprecedented crisis, a crisis of definition. What is a human being when she has lost her erotic center? And where is that center? In the heart, the genitals, culture, writing?

In "Dear Ovid," Alison Fell goes into the past to draw out a healing love song that will help put her broken lover back together. Her poem of loss is redolent with animal desire, it rings with pain, it recalls winter, the weight of mammalian sorrow, the heat of spring-wakened beasts, the shapes of nature's indifference, old rifts between wanderers and nesters. Her song recapitulates the classic lament of Penelope, but is addressed to Ovid, the political exile, not to Odysseus, the adventurer. In the end, it does not matter. The poetry remains, but the lover is gone. The excursion into the past, into literature, did not help. Had this powerful song been sung in Africa it might have worked. In the West, the gods are too far away. There is too big a tear between nature and writing. The weaving is in crisis. But writing helps little: "Such grief robs us of all syntax; our dreams are stricken, we do not know what we have become. In disorder we get up each day, and in disorder we lie down."

I once climbed atop an allegorical statue depicting the state of Iowa, for a television documentary. I cupped Iowa's patinaed breasts, giving off their bounty, and grinned for the camera. Some such activity takes place in Sandro Zanotto's allegorical tale, "The Hermit's Manuscript." The slightly worn, excitingly tarnished, uncertain-aged trollop who resides on the hermit's boat is none other than Italia, the Patria herself. A made-up Venetian courtesan who needs her masks and her sex games to arouse her lover, she is nonetheless everything a modern Italian might understand by patriotism: mother, infantile sexuality, docility, and willing perversity. Unlike Mother Russia, whose grief is without guile, Courtesan Italy can permit herself the luxuries of irony and fantasy.

At the same time, this story, written by a man, best illustrates, albeit in an extreme way, the difference in sexual outlook between men and women. Men, like the Hermit, will allow themselves to desacralize sex with humor, thereby de-eroticizing it. Women, almost never: for them sex is primordial, sacramental, serious. For the reader, too, the erotic best works seriously. The literary form of the erotic story is kin to the fairy tale: it demands a suspension of disbelief, a deliberate purging of all worlds except its own.

Western Europe reaches its farthest sexual shore in Portugal, the westernmost shore of Europe. The unhappy, middle-aged, abstinent homosexual in Richard Zimler's "Unholy Ghosts" finds sex and love in exile. Portugal is a pre-AIDS paradise, a province as yet uncorrupted by the plague. Ironically, in the very act of discovering sex, love, innocence, and an idyllic past, he destroys it by his very presence. The bitter lesson here is that the sexually and politically repressed Third World may yet become a Disneyland for moneyed Westerners, a perverse parody of our own "innocent" past. *Et in Arcadia simulacrum.*

But the opposite is quite possible, too, at least in fiction. What if the displaced colonials who now stream into the capitals of Europe reverse the traditional relationship of master and slave, object and subject? This is what Cameroonian exile Calixthe Beyala tells in her story of sadomasochism in Paris, *Her Touch.* in a play reminiscent of Jean Genêt's *The Maids* and Frantz Fanon's *Black Skin, White Masks,* the young African factory worker makes her boss her sexual slave. She then proceeds to enslave his former mistresses and thus conquers the means of (re)production. The sex-bursting Cameroonian embodies the white men and women's fantasies of the uninhibited savage. Ironically, in order to learn just what an uninhibited savage is, she studies the whores on Pigalle. The whores, of course, know every game, come in every color, and understand the economic basis for the sexual transaction. But conquering the world through smart sex doesn't lead to contentment, only to disgust. "What a terrible nightmare," the conqueror exclaims, "to live in a world covered with white cunt-juice."

The world of the African exile in the European capital is complemented in Maryse Condé's "No Woman Cry," about a former exile who returns home. Letitia has come back to tropical Guadeloupe to reclaim a place in her parents' village. Her big-city sexual persona horrifies the villagers who have intricate mores for inhabiting the immensely sen-

sual tropic. In a sense, the natives have built protection against the se-
ductive environment. But Letitia feels it all, the velvety night, the sweat
on a man's muscular back, the knotted roots of the big trees, the mois-
ture in the night, the headiness of flowers. She feels it doubly strong,
both as childhood memory and as a European slumming in the tropics.
Her passion ends up centering, not unexpectedly, on another stranger,
a black American.

In René Depèstre's "The Enchantment of an Hour of Rain," the mys-
teries of mixing, creolization, exile, travel, and sex merge for an illuminated afternoon orgy in a stormy Rio de Janeiro. A black Brazilian
man and two white women join on Ipanema during a storm. They make
a mythic beast together, denying in a single act taboos of both race and
sex.

The ultimate mix of urban exile-cum-fin-de-siècle-wanderlust-gumbo
occurs in "Ecstasy," a story by the Japanese Ryu Murakami. Two lovers
meet in a neon-lit Tokyo that could also be New York, Paris, or Berlin.
It's the international, delocalized melting pot. At first, they aren't sure
whether they even want to sleep with each other. But then they take Ecstasy, a drug that makes all their alienation vanish as if by magic. The
drug brings them back home in their bodies at a level of intimacy that
not even the most isolated culture on earth can achieve. They are swept
along biological paths that commune with the very beginnings of the universe. And all this in an impersonal, though expensive, hotel room in
Tokyo. The magic joining of these lovers is neither ironic nor deserved.
They are inhabiting a purely new global reality where the details of nationality, cultural difference, even gender, have disappeared. We are in
the transnational superstate of sheer biological drive.

The ironies and reversals in the work of exiles, returnees, and no-
mads may represent a new form of sexuality. Instead of being alienat-
ing, their experiences may be cross-pollinating, as they are for Depèstre.
In a world where we can no longer keep our secrets, we can no longer
be provincial. Encounters with the perspectives of people from every
part of the globe can help reconnect us to ourselves.

Regarding sex, every culture cultivates degrees of indirection. The
approaches to speaking about desire are forms of flirtation that eventually, as one becomes more intimate, become forms of seduction and
then, in extremis, sexual positions. The approaches to the subject mirror the approaches to the body. They also mirror a culture's view of itself.

For Europeans, sex and writing have achieved a position that is weirdly similar to that of the Mandarin Chinese. Writing matters inordinately to Westerners floundering in oversignified postmodernity. For some, sex is a life jacket that, on close inspection, turns out to be made of words. The lovers in Annie Ernaux's "Paper Traces of Philippe V" become truly animated when they make love on a large sheet of drawing paper on which their menses and sperm mingle to make art. "There are only two essential things in my life—writing and making love. I can only transcribe those moments in which such a link strikes me as obvious . . ." claims the narrator.

In Carole Maso's "The Women Who Wash Lentils," language is the heroine of the whole love story. "When she is French, and she slowly opens the legs of the woman she also opens the book and reads. . . ." The lovers engender and arouse each other with readings from two books, which turn out to have been written by the author herself. The writer masturbates to invent and invents to masturbate the reader. What she invents is also what she has read, so that the referential universe of female sex teems with salt, waves, mollusks, animals, breath, and other women writer-lovers such as Anaïs Nin and Kay Boyle. Even invention then turns out to be remembrance of things read.

The sexual globe short-circuits at this writerly extreme.

Berrigan Back in Print: Rejoice

At long last, the works of my master and teacher, Ted Berrigan, are back in print. Penguin Books brought out *The Selected Poems of Ted Berrigan,* an event that sends a shiver of delight through his devotees. Ted Berrigan was the poetic guru of my generation. Like Socrates, he taught in the agora, in this case the corner of Second Avenue and St. Mark's Place, where he could be often found, with a rolled-up *New York Times* under his arm, smoking a Chesterfield with a long ash that threatened to end up in his beard—it often did.

When I could barely speak English, he taught me American. He pointed out what was specifically American in the poetry he championed, and he told me whom to read, especially his own masters, Frank

O'Hara and Jack Kerouac. Ted lived and made poetry twenty-four hours a day because he never seemed to sleep. The best time to see him was four A.M., when he shined most brightly in his apartment at 101 St. Mark's Place.

When he died, his books were barely available, probably because most of them were published by small presses and their runs were quickly exhausted. From the midsixties until the midseventies, American poetry underwent a splendid transformation, leaving the staid pages of academic quarterlies and taking residence on the streets and in coffeehouses. This transformation had in Ted Berrigan an immensely educated watchdog who made sure that the exciting populism was also formally brilliant and that the American language, which he loved, was furthered.

After he died, the excitement of the art seemed to die too: it retreated between the faux-ivory (plastic, really) walls of MFA programs. But suddenly, America is once more in the throes of a poetic revolution: the coffeehouses are full of young poets, bardic contests rock the bars, the human voice leaps off the page, and the street corners ring once more with red-hot language. And, appropriately, Ted Berrigan's poems are back in print.

I **Fell** into the **Hands** of the French

It started out innocently enough. A group of American writers were going to host a distinguished French poet for a week and translate one of his poems. What could be more harmless? A beautiful hotel in New Orleans, poets seated around a table, mineral water and wine. Ah, but poesy has mysterious ways. Slowly, slowly, the exercise of translating the high romantic verses of our host began to take on the hellish tint of labor in the mines of the underworld.

First, there were the words themselves, the meanings of which, even if it were possible to fathom them, did not cross willingly from one language into another. Take *"crevisse,"* for instance, which could be "crevasse," "chasm," "fissure," or "crack." Each translator was partial to a different vision of that *"crevisse."* My left-hand neighbor, being of a gloomy disposition, was enamored of "chasm." At my right, there was a push for "fissure." Myself, I went for "crack." The poet himself, elegant and still like a marmorean rendition of the Poet himself, hovered bemusedly over the proceedings, proffering now and then some subtle essence of thought. In this case, he pronounced that if we used the word *crack* we might be accused of drug propaganda. Everyone came briefly down from the lyric ether for this, but soon we ascended again.

No two words seemed to pass easily over from French into English, a resistance that could be attributed to the fact that in French there are fewer words than in English, thus making each one a trifle more precious. The poem itself, like the poet, offered no compromises: it soared relentlessly on the back of a bruised female figure, which had done the same job for hundreds of French poets before. After five eight-hour days of this attempt to steer the recalcitrant French muse into the pragmatic confines of American directness, I ran screaming out of the translation chamber convinced that 1, no one should ever translate anything—it's easier to learn the original language, and 2, the reason I escaped Communism was that groups such as these awaited me as soon as I looked old enough to suffer.

Dr. Alphabet

*T*he Adventures of Dr. Alphabet, by
Dave Morice, is subtitled *104 Unusual Ways to Write Poetry in the
Classroom and the Community.* It is my belief that if Dr. Alphabet's
recipes were followed, many of our nation's problems would be solved.

Take, for instance, the blindfold poem. In 1977, Dr. Alphabet wrote
blindfolded for ten hours at an art festival in New Hope, Pennsylvania.
He became, he tells us, "more aware of sounds, smells, and conversations." Wouldn't it be wonderful if we had a national "writing blindfolded" day? Nobody would be using his or her computer consoles, just
their noses, their ears, and their fingers.

Another of the doctor's ideas is the poetry shirt, where you write on
your shirt or your friends' shirts. This is not like buying a preprinted

shirt with words from the factory: this is your very own poetry on your very own shirt. Nobody can get you like they are trying to get Pamela O'Leary in Michigan for her license plate that says 4RU486, which is the name of the French abortion drug. In that case, the state gave her the license and now the state wants it back. On your poetry shirt you give yourself license and nobody, if I'm not mistaken, can take the shirt off your back, except for the IRS, of course.

Dr. Alphabet also recommends making a Rolodex poem. Every day you write different lines of poetry on the cards in your Rolodex: in about a year you have a lot of poems you can flip through when you want to read something. Isn't that a whole lot better than flipping through your Rolodex as you do now and finding only the depressing names of ex-friends, failed business partners, and people you don't remember at all?

I can't list here all of Dr. Alphabet's ideas, but here are a few, quickly: Spiderweb of Words, Poetry Wooden Nickels, Verse Tubes, Letter Galaxy, Cartoon Cards. The best part is you don't have to be a kid to play. Change your life with Dr. Alphabet!

Swimming Between Languages

The world's getting both bigger and smaller at the same time. Television will give us the illusion that we are familiar with a faraway place just because we see some shadows moving under a vaguely unfamiliar tree canopy. Airplanes are making us believe that distance is irrelevant, that geography is just some blurred lines far below. Telephones transport our voices erasing the swamps, rivers, woods, subdivisions, military bases, and toxic pits that surely lie between. E-mail and faxing are jetting our disembodied thoughts instantaneously through hyperspace.

But for all that, we seem to know less and less about each other. More and more, in this postmodern, postmortem, post-cereal world, we are allowing our electronic illusion makers, particularly television, to tell our stories for us.

The stories television tells us are by no means "our" stories. Not only are we becoming too lazy to tell our stories but, under the simpleminded assault of programmed pixels, we are actually *forgetting* our stories. Human beings today are bereft of stories, robbed of stories, impoverished.

The telling of stories and the question of what we remember and what we forget are fundamental to the business of teaching English to people from other languages and other cultures.

Many of us take English around the world into people's homes, so we become the chief storytellers of American culture. It is obvious that now, after the tearing of the so-called Iron Curtain, the thirst for English in the world has increased tenfold. English has become synonymous with economic progress, democracy, and scientific advancement.

But while this may well be true, the job of artists and teachers is to transmit the poetry of our language and the stories of our culture. While the world is mesmerized by our technology, it feels quite ambiguous about our culture. To many people around the world, American culture is what they know from Hollywood and TV in foreign syndication. People around the world are familiar with such American archetypes as J.R. and Matlock, to name only two characters wildly popular in Eastern Europe.

Many people in the world feel threatened, quite rightly, by the flood of American films and music, products which are technically superior but morally and emotionally quite deficient. It isn't very hard to figure out why our pop culture exerts such fascination for young people in other countries: they picture a glossy, Technicolor world of plenty in which violence and sex lead to facile solutions to all problems. Given the real-life difficulties in people's day-to-day lives, such palliatives are powerful. The American entertainment industry thus perpetuates the time-honored vision of America as a utopia for the daring, the uprooted, the reckless, the adventurer. This has been the fundamental lure of America since the nineteenth century and perhaps before.

The only problem with this picture is that it's mostly wrong. America may still be a land of opportunity but our day-to-day life is no less complex, emotionally challenging, ambiguous, and uncertain than the life of people elsewhere. The truth of this dailiness, the simple truth of our lives, can only be told by us, the storytellers in English. Our job is to tell the stories that Hollywood and TV do not tell. This is, of course, a tall order, given the fact that many of us are as entranced by the glittery fictions of our electronic masters as the poorest peasants of the Andes. Still, there is no one else. We must tell our stories to the rest of the world, a job that involves the awesome, preparatory task of actually remembering these stories. And also remembering the ways in which they differ from the glossy fictions.

Talk about difficulty: we have to teach the language of the future while interpreting a present and past that are at odds with the cartoon future of our propaganda.

For all that, I am not a nostalgist or a conservative. While our films and songs present an unrealistic view of this country, they are also powerful agents of change. Native cultures are not all good: in many cases they are filled with elements of discord, chauvinism, a historically defensive outlook, nationalist propaganda, and irrational calls to battle. Sure, the music is beautiful, the costumes are gorgeous, the cheese festival an olfactory delight, but hidden within these picturesque elements you can also glimpse the corpses of thousands of years of useless conflict. Folk music and dance are a hell of a lot prettier in, let's say, Salt Lake City, where a multicultural ensemble has isolated the esthetic from the murderous.

At the same time, the unadorned folk cultures and life-styles of the genuine and unglamorous teach us a complexity that we have all but forgotten. Languages teach such complexity as well because the history and culture they embody is the sum total of what people have learned in their history.

It only makes sense then that as we teach English and tell our stories we must also learn the native languages and listen to the stories they tell us. The future is born at the intersection of one another's stories.

My own story is that of an immigrant to the United States.

When someone first comes to America, the most urgent task is the telling of one's story. One needs to communicate urgently, at the most profound yet most immediate level, the story of where one comes from, the story of who one is. This is necessary in order to reestablish a sense of self, to build a new self, if you will, to bridge the differences between one's old universe and the new one. Words are merely pointers, and what they point to may or may not be what they appear to mean. What is certain is that they point outward to one's life and surroundings and that is where their usefulness lies.

(This, you may note, is directly opposed to that teaching, which maintains that words point inward to a self-referential universe of signs that can be logically and grammatically taught.)

On the surface, it may seem that what your immigrant needs to know is how to get directions, how to shop, how to find a job, how to get an education, but in effect those necessities are only aspects of the need to tell one's story. When an immigrant says, "I want a cup of coffee," what he or she is saying is: "I"—an "I" that is not the same as the former *"Yo," "Je,"* or *"Eu"*—would like to tell the "you" that an American cup—not the same as *"taza," "tasse,"* or *"ceasca"*—is wanted. "Coffee"—which is not *"café," "cafeaua,"* or *"cave"*—is the code for an entire tradition. The story he or she needs to tell is that an "I" born in a landscape much different from this, once drank a cup of coffee in a world where a "cup of coffee" signified intimacy, talk, a certain atmosphere, perhaps sophistication, or a certain style of leisure and reflection. What surrounds this request is the plea for an opening to tell the story of one's differences.

My own "cup of coffee" occurred in Detroit when I was but two months out of Europe. I kept wandering aimlessly through the city, looking for the "center." In Europe, cities are built around a center where one finds the urban civilization: stores, movie theaters, coffeehouses. The European city center cannot be translated as "downtown," since many American cities' business districts are not necessarily created for human comfort and pleasure. And what's more, sadly, even these approximate downtown centers have been abandoned in many cities, like Detroit. What I didn't know, as I kept walking past vast, burned-out industrial wastes, and oddly silent and frightened neighborhoods, was that American cities, with a few exceptions like New Orleans, were built for the automobile, not for strolling pedestrians.

At long last, I entered a coffee shop in a black neighborhood. A waitress was wiping the counter with a rag, an old black man was leaning against ancient jukebox, and a pie plate was revolving slowly near the cash register, with three slices missing. I said, "Café, please." The waitress didn't understand me. The man by the jukebox came over and the three of us conferred. The problem was quickly solved, but then there remained the question of milk and sugar. "Black," I said, pointing to the waitress, meaning "like you." Well, that could have been a touchy moment if I hadn't been such an obviously sincere foreigner. They both burst out laughing and the man by the jukebox ended up explaining to me with great animated delight that he himself prefered his coffee "white like me," and he poked me with his finger to make his point.

I stayed there about four hours, having about eight cups of coffee, until closing time. My new pal, Marcus, took me over to a neighborhood bar after that where he played the jukebox and explained at great length the importance of the songs we were listening to. I can remember the songs to this day though we had switched from coffee to gin, but the explanations that went with the songs were perfectly incomprehensible to me. But, guess what? I had found the center of the city of Detroit: it was situated at the intersection of two stories that met each other somehow, over a misunderstanding.

Misunderstanding, mishearing, and mistranslating are often more powerful learning tools than accuracy. It is when one makes a mistake that the gap through which stories poke their head opens. Not to mention the fact that such misunderstandings make pretty good post-facto stories. For instance, I used to confuse the words "buy" and "ride" for some reason. I once boarded the Dexter bus in Detroit and asked the driver, "Can I buy the Dexter bus?" "I don't think so," he replied, "but you could try buying the Livernois bus."

A while later I fell in love with the songs of Bob Dylan and decided to write down the words that so impressed me. I faithfully transcribed thirty songs. One day I showed them to a friend who laughed until he had tears in his eyes. It turned out that I hadn't gotten a single word right. My songs were by no means Dylan's. Dare I say it? They were better. One day I will publish a book: *Thirty Bob Dylan Songs by Andrei Codrescu.*

I consider myself most fortunate for having arrived in the United States without speaking a word of English. I learned the language by osmosis, absorbing the words with the entire repertoire of gestures, body language, place, context, and emphasis. Words are only a small part in the vocabulary of human communication.

We all know stories about people who came to America speaking perfect English only to find themselves perfectly at sea. I knew a Romanian in Baltimore who had studied psychiatry at the University of Bucharest. He was working as an intern at Shepherd-Pratt, a psychiatric hospital, and becoming increasingly despondent over his inability to communicate with his patients, many of whom had linguistic disorders. Heck, he couldn't even communicate with the opposite sex. He had a nervous breakdown and ended up doing time at Shepherd-

Pratt as a patient. What broke him down was all the unspoken language that surrounds and permeates the spoken.

When I came to America I had an urgent need to communicate because I was nineteen years old and I had a few things I had to tell girls right away. I wasn't all that interested in things like "Today we went to the supermarket. Dogs were on sale." Eventually, I did just that, and learned more English than patient schooling would have ever succeeded in teaching me.

Now, no matter how well it may seem to you that I speak English, my English is not the kind that can be taught in school. It is accented English, an English infused by my native Romanian. This is not to say that Romanian syntax or actual words modify my English, but that my original language seeks out in English precisely those qualities that are most like itself. English and Romanian are vastly different languages. Romanian is more poetic, metaphorical, often onomatopoeic, whereas English is more precise, factual, informative. Beyond a certain rudimentary utility, Romanians and Americans speak for different reasons. Romanians talk in order to experience intimacy, community, the pleasure of the words themselves. What is said is not so important as how it is said or the fact that talking is taking place. By contrast, Americans like to communicate information. Beyond that, chatter, banter, and gossip are generally acknowledged to be the province of women while it is considered unseemly for men to indulge in those seemingly gratuitous uses. Another exception may be black culture, which has rap, jive, and other oral forms that hark back to an ancient orality. The feeling that underlies the Romanians' pleasure in speech is one of generosity, of waste, of expansiveness, and the belief, perhaps, that words are the only things plentifully available. Unlike cheese, meat, and potatoes, let's say. Americans who, quite the contrary, have too much meat, eggs, and potatoes, are stingy with words. They seem to be saving them for something. I'm talking, of course, about real people now, not about the paste of words and endless buzz that pours out of mechanical contraptions everywhere.

The fact is, however, that no language can be truly learned outside of the ways in which people squander, save, and actually speak words.

No language ever stuck to me in school. By the age of six, before I even went to school, I had already forgotten two languages. I spoke Hungarian with my grandmother, German with my mother, and Romanian with the kids on my street. These languages were completely interchangeable and seemed "natural" to the point where I never even noticed that I switched from one language to another. I didn't even know that they were separate languages. After I started going to school, which was taught in Romanian, I forgot both Hungarian and German, above a certain rudimentary level.

In school we had Russian and French. In four years I didn't learn a word of Russian because I was in love with my Russian teacher, Comrade Papadopolou, who wore the first miniskirt in Eastern Europe. I didn't hear a word she said. French was taught by a very strict pedagogue of the old school who corrected misconjugation with a ruler rap across the knuckles. In his presence, I conjugated automatically anything that came to mind, and later, when I went to France, I couldn't keep myself from conjugating. If I said to someone, *"J'ai faim,"* my mind would immediately start *"tu as faim, il a faim, nous avons faim, vous avez faim, ils ont faim."* It's a good thing I didn't stay in France, in the tradition of other Romanian writers, or I'd be a nervous wreck.

Now the first American word I learned, while I was still in Romania, was "Coca-Cola." My friend Ion and I had an argument. He said that Coca-Cola was a nonalcoholic drink while I maintained that it was a powerful alcohol. We pooled our resources and entered one of Bucharest's best hotels, bellied up to the bar, and ordered Coca-Cola. The two glasses of Coke cost as much as we had. After we had sipped them judiciously, Ion declared that he felt no effect. I, on the other hand, got quite drunk.

"Coffee" is by no means *"café,"* just as "house" is not *"maison,"* though they may translate similarly. A foreign language isn't just words. It is another view of the world. A French house is not an American house. They are built differently, look different, have a different history, are inhabited differently. Because of this, it is nearly impossible to learn a language without knowing the place and the people who speak it. Words come with gestures, gestures come with landscapes. Words are alive, inhabited.

In teaching English to people from elsewhere we ought to tailor this teaching to opening us to them and them to us. We ought to teach them the phrases and gestures that allow for the passage of their stories into our world and for the passage of our stories into theirs. Naturally, this is best accomplished by taking them to dinner or to bed, or by walking around, taking buses, engaging strangers, going to cafés, visiting jails and mental hospitals. Some of this may be dangerous, which is good. Danger is a powerful incentive to learning.

Second, we ought to cultivate mistakes, misunderstanding, and mishearing in our teaching. Instead of immediately correcting these apparent mistakes we ought to enlarge upon them until cracks large enough appear to allow for the pouring forth of stories (though these may be merely gestural). In an ideal world, I would advocate the purposeful teaching of mistakes, thus allowing the students to discover the consequences in the real world. For instance, if we were to teach them that the word for "coffee" is "tea," that the word for "floor" is "ceiling" and so on, the results would be the creation of not just speakers of English, but creative producers of it. The resulting confusion would give birth to metaphors our culture sorely needs.

Third, I would encourage the teaching of English through poetic phrases that do not resemble in the least those to be found in texts today. For instance, Rimbaud's phrase "oxidize the gargoyles" could be proffered to the students for them to go out into the world and find a use for it. Not only will they end up providing a meaning to this still-mysterious injunction, but some of them may become meta-architects. This method has the advantage of providing us with something in return for our pains, namely some "meaning," and the enlargement of the job market through the creation of novel occupations. There are no "gargoyle oxidizers" presently listed in the U.S. Labor Department's *Book of Jobs.*

Incidentally, "poet" is listed in there as some kind of low-paying, white-collar job, unfortunately. I liked it better when poets weren't listed.

Language is only one player in an area of communication that contains a multitude of them. I believe, along with certain biolinguists that we have an innate sense of language. At some fundamental level all languages share a universal structure. When we teach English we are only teaching the sounds and symbols of a difference that is perfectly within the grasp of anyone already having language.

Children are, happily, greatly superior to adults in the facility of learning that difference. They are also much better mimics and, because they love to play, they can easily twist their tongues and scrunch up their faces in order to produce new sounds.

It is important, I think, to play. Languages create their own physiognomies. The French have different faces from the Americans because of the way their sounds shape their mouths and their skulls. The varied physiognomies and different emotional expressions of speakers of different languages are a marvelous illustration of the stories contained by those languages. Even if you don't speak Russian, all you have to do is read Dostoyevski to get that sultry, slightly bitter expression Russians have when they are having coffee at the Russian Tea Room. Stories can rearrange your face even in translation.

No two animals make the same sounds in any language, which indicates that the stories are different, too. The ability of children to imitate is only surpassed by their thirst for stories. What's more, the kind of stories that children grasp quickly and effectively—fairy tales, myths, legends, fables—are nearly contemporaneous with the birth of the languages in which they are told. Onomatopoeia often determines the direction of these stories.

Adults are another matter. They have had time to kill their imaginations in their native tongue, and it is difficult for them to be born again. Many of them are not so keen on telling their stories either. Wars, revolutions, slaughter, famine, and hunger, are, more often than not, the experience they have left behind. They have no taste for recalling it. Most people, since the nineteenth century, have come to America to escape from their homelands. Some of them would like to forget even the languages of the places where they came from. Russian Jews escaping pogroms in the 1890s did not much care to speak Russian after they got here. Come to think of it, they didn't much care to speak it in Russia.

When dealing with adults we should carefully assess what their attitude toward their own stories is. Clearly, a teenager who may not have had a terrible life is a lot more eager to tell his or her budding protostory than a former inmate of the Gulag.

Still, even such people have an enormous store of stories that they can and will eagerly tell. These are the stories of their civilized moments, the stories of their cooking, the stories of their wedding rituals, the fairy tales of their childhood. If we give them an opportunity to tell these, they will blossom. They might even play.

Brâncuşi

Fiarele
se văietau
lemnele
se-ncovoiau,
văile
îmi răsunau
pietrele
se despicau
şi codrii
se clătinau
se jelea
într-un cuvînt
toată firea
pe pămînt

(*Naramza a Frumoă, Basme Române*, G. Dem. Teodorescu, Editura Litera, 1965).

Let me a try a pale translation of this lament from the Romanian fairy tale "Beautiful Naramza."

The beasts were wailing
the wood
was bending
the valleys
echoed for me
the stones
were cleaved
and the forests
swayed:
in a word
all being
on this earth
mourned

The only thing lost in this translation is the poetry, which is to say, almost everything. But not everything. What remains is all of Constantin Brâncuşi's subjects and materials. The beasts are here, all of them: the magic birds, the rooster, the seal, the fish, the penguins, the walking and flying turtle, even the chilling nocturnal creature. And here also are his materials: wood and stone. Together, these beasts and these materials form a single substance called being. The woods and the stones are moved by the same vital force as the animals, and this force is sympathy. In this fairy tale, the being of all that is created laments two human deaths. The first is the death of Naramza's mother, which so upsets her daughter, Naramza, that her heart breaks, causing the being of the world to lament in sympathy. The second death is Naramza's own, for whom nature grieves again. But Naramza comes back to life and nature rejoices: she is truly one of them. She dies and is reborn just like the leaves and the buds.

The beasts in fairy tales do not have faces. They are moved by sympathy with one another, by forces that we can intuit but not see. Human heroes of tales are handicapped by their tools and by the weight of their social conventions. They need the help of animals to find their mates, to find sympathy and happiness. When the *Măiastra* (Magic Bird) helps Ileana Consînzeana find *Făt Frumos* (Handsome Lad, her beloved) she does so because she is an *ur*-bird, an archetypical kin of the lovers, an ancestor. She uses language because humans do, but language is just another noise in a vast repertoire of them. Other magic birds, ants, turtles, bees, and seals, help the escapes of heroes by lending them their essence. Birds help heroes fly, ants burrow tunnels for them, bees raise walls of honey. The pursuers are snared and misled by these animal essences. Sometimes these essences are used paradoxically: birds walk instead of flying, while turtles fly.

In 1956, the Philadelphia Museum of Art, turned Brâncuşi's *Turtle* upside down. It was originally supposed to be seen the other way, with the shell up and the flat side down, like any old turtle. For some reason, it was exhibited the other way, the rounded part down, the flat part up. Brâncuşi saw a photograph of this and was amused. "Now my turtle is flying," he said. And it has been shown that way ever since.

Two things strike me about this. First, Brâncuşi enjoyed the paradox because it brought his turtle even closer to the turtle in fairy tales which is the closest one could possibly get to an *ur*-turtle; second, he allowed for the play of chance to enter his work, something one might think uncharacteristic, given his precision and his insistence on just the right way to see his work. The first points to Brâncuşi's deeply felt insight that no matter how close one might get to the perfection of an ideal form, one is never close enough, therefore never finished. The second is that Brâncuşi was not a stuffed shirt: he was a modern, a friend of both Marcel Duchamp and Tristan Tzara, his compatriot, who founded Dada.

On occasion he could be both a Platonist and a Dadaist. At the exhibition of the Society of Independent Artists in New York in 1917, Brâncuşi exhibited his *Sculpture for the Blind,* which consisted of one of his marble eggs, an ovoid sculpture enclosed in a bag that had two sleeves through which the spectator could put his hands to feel it. This Independent Artists' exhibition was also where Marcel Duchamp entered his infamous *R. Mutt* urinal. Brâncuşi's egg was Dada both by design and by association. At the same time, it *was* a sculpture for the blind because it was intended to be felt, not seen.

Tristan Tzara was a Jewish poet from Moineşti, Moldavia, Romania. The Dada movement, possibly the first international art movement, owes much to Tzara's Romanian roots, namely a keen sense of the absurd, a wicked sense of humor, and a profound conviction that the world is not what it seems to be. In the Balkans the world never coincided with its official description, a fact that is present in folk tales, in proverbs, in absurd humor. Also present in the provincial caldron of Bucharest before World War I were at least two self-conscious literary and artistic tendencies: a European-looking, dandified, fashion-conscious art and a protofascist folklorism.

The small Bucharest avant-garde at the start of the century was contemptuous of both these pseudocultures. Folklore was infinitely more varied and complex than nationalists believed. The natural world and the humans in folk and fairy tales were in touch with something more primordial and deeper than some manufactured national identity. The stories of the world's first absurdist writer, Urmuz, follow both the logic of fairy tales and the dream logic of an alienated urbanite. Fairy tales contained a strong antidote to bourgeois rationalism. A mystical inclination runs through Tristan Tzara and Victor Brauner's work. Brauner, a friend and contemporary of Tzara, was also Romanian and Jewish. Both of them came from a Jewish religious world that had its own rich store of folklore as well as mystical traditions. Dada absorbed and rejected all of these influences on its way to world revolution.

The world of pre–World War I Europe was encrusted with pretension, heavy with posturing, sentimentality, decoration, pomposity, and bureaucratic formality. Even on the verge of collapse, Europe continued pretending nothing was wrong. Artists were first to ring the alarms and to puncture the self-important facade. The Dada movement did so resolutely and to great effect, both by ridiculing the existing conventions and by creating art objects and writings that were unlike anything ever seen. Man Ray's spiked iron and Marcel Duchamp's toilet were such critical works, both commentary and illustration.

While not an active participant in the Dada revolution, the work of Constantin Brâncuşi was also revolutionary. But while the Dadaists were social critics as well as artists, Brâncuşi was all artist. He pursued a philosophical quest that was, implicitly, critical of academic art, but was, above all, mystical and rigorously formal. Dada responded to decorative excess with Dadaist excess. Brâncuşi tried to exorcise excess in order to reveal the essential forms. He did this by drawing both from his roots and from the artistic revolution that gave birth to modern art.

The question of whether Brâncuşi was more Romanian carver than Parisian art revolutionary is a chicken-and-egg question. He was undoubtedly Romanian because he drew many of his forms from the folk art of his native place. His menagerie, with the exception of the penguins, comes from Romanian fairy tales. His effacing of individual features of faces has its source in Byzantine icons. His *Infinite Column* has prototypes in Oltenian porch supports. His *Chimera* resembles the masks worn by Christmas carolers. His decorative motifs can be seen to issue from the family house and church at Hobiţa and from the carved dowry chests of the region. The *Table of Silence* originates in the low, round dining table found in Oltenian peasant homes, the so-called *masa joasă*. Or one can trace it to rural millstones, some of which he kept in his studio. Perhaps, most Romanian and most paradoxical of all his work is the ensemble of monuments at Tîrgu-Jiu, Romania, consisting of the *Infinite Column*, the *Gate of the Kiss*, the *Table of Silence*, and several hourglass seats. This construction, which commemorates a battle site, distorts Brâncuşi's simplicity, sending it off into the heroic, a kind of pomposity generally belied by his work.

Still, at Tîrgu-Jiu, Brâncuşi brought back to Romania everything he had learned abroad, and thus completed a circle. He brought back his roots, after having stretched them to encompass the world. Paradoxically, Brâncuşi became more Romanian the longer he stayed away. It is as if the same process that led him to pare his stone down to essentials led him to his own essence.

But without Paris, without New York and Philadelphia, without Rodin, Picasso, Satie, Duchamp, Walter Arensberg, Peggy Guggenheim, Nancy Cunard, without his encounters with African sculpture, without exile, such return would not have been possible. Apollinaire, upon first seeing his work in 1912, wrote that Brâncuşi was "a delicate and very personal sculptor whose works have great refinement." Brâncuşi had by then been in Paris for eight years. Paris, the art capital of Europe, and New York and Philadelphia, where his patrons were, made Brâncuşi's artistic discoveries possible. Consider just the path to one of his great works, *Portrait of Nancy Cunard*, 1925–27 and 1928–32. Nancy Cunard, the granddaughter of the founder of the Cunard ship company, was the Paris publisher of Samuel Beckett and Ezra Pound. She was introduced to Brâncuşi in 1924 by her friend Tristan Tzara. The sculpture itself is a classic Brâncuşi featureless female form, but with the extraordinary whimsy of some kind of twisted roll on top of it, a pleated bread perhaps, of the kind Romanians call *cozonac*, or, more likely, some sort of insouciant chignon. With that addition, Brâncuşi paid homage to the entire chain of circumstances that had brought him Nancy Cunard, without ceasing for a moment to conduct his researches into form. I have not read much on Brâncuşi's whimsy, sense of humor, irony, or pleasure in paradox, but these, too, are constants in his work. He shares these qualities with the greats of his age: Apollinaire, Picasso, Satie, Tzara, Brauner, Duchamp. What is extraordinary is that these utterly modern, if not postmodern qualities, seem almost incidental to the evidently serious, transcendental labor of his art. About Brâncuşi we say, "He was a mystic who also spoke the vulgate," while about Duchamp we say, "He spoke such exquisite vulgate he had to be a mystic."

Marcel Duchamp was Brâncuşi's friend, his agent in America, and the owner of several of his works. Brâncuşi's early success in America allowed him the independence he needed to work at his own pace. He had no need to produce hack work after American collectors took an interest. He said it himself: "Without the Americans, I would not have been able to produce all this or even to have existed."

Few of the clichés about Brâncuşi are wrong, especially when they seem contradictory. He was a Danubian peasant, a Carpathian sage, an Oriental seer, an alchemist, a saint of Montparnasse, an admirer of African art, an occultist, a lover of beautiful women, a primitive, a sophisticate, a diplomat, and a child. He also had a real dog, Polaire, whom he never sculpted, a nameless rooster, whom he sculpted several times. He was both the heir to Michelangelo, whom he bad-mouthed, and a village carver. His first *Mademoiselle Poganys are* phallic, as either Picasso or Matisse observed, thereby causing a scandal, and his phallic Adam in *Adam and Eve* is sacramental. Paradox and contradiction are intrinsic to his art, which is an effort to reconcile opposites. He said, "Beauty is absolute balance." For there to be balance there has to be tension between opposites. In his ovoids, Brâncuşi arrived at the creation of the world. And on the curvature of those perfectly balanced cosmic eggs, contradictions coexist.

Brâncuşi's occult side was well nourished by theosophy and alchemical discussions. *Coincidentia oppositorum* was the currency of such doctrines. He drew from Plato and Ovid, but he doubtless had read the modern metaphysical poets Rainer Maria Rilke, Stefan George, and his own compatriot and admirer, Lucian Blaga.

About *Măiastra* (The Bird), Blaga wrote:

> *Are you a bird*
> *a travelling bell*
> *Or a creature, an earless jug perhaps?*
> *A golden song spinning*
> *above our fear of dead riddles?*

Blaga was ideally suited to question the Bird because his poetry issued from the same depths of folklore and metaphysical longing as

Brâncuşi's. Blaga's first book was called *Poems of the Light*. Brâncuşi's ovoids are alchemical eggs, those radiant objects that gave birth to matter and new light. He was able to see through the light to the essential forms under appearances. Blaga said, "We are hidden in the light," and that ambiguous maxim could have been said by Brâncuşi. The world is hidden in the light and by the light. We are blind when we can see and we can see when we are blind. Hence, *Sculpture for the Blind*. The transparency of Brâncuşi's work is what most makes it mysterious. But neither transparency nor simplicity was his goal.

"Simplicity is not an end in art, but one arrives at simplicity in spite of oneself, in approaching the real sense of things. Simplicity is at bottom complexity and one must be nourished on its essence to understand its significance." (1926)

What is "the real sense of things"? A mystery certainly, but not a fiction. Brâncuşi needed, as did most of his contemporaries, including the Dadaists, to remove those constructs which the world uses to obscure that "real sense of things." But unlike some of these other moderns, he did not find an absurd, bottomless pit whenever he stripped away another layer. He did indeed get to the real sense of things. As for being nourished by the essence of simplicity, Brâncuşi was nourished by his peasant childhood and by the carving art of village craftsmen. His village and his childhood were his simplicity, but it took all the sophisticated tools of Paris and the radical deconstruction of the world by the others for this simplicity to be realized.

In speaking of contradictions, paradoxes, the union of opposites, and so on, we should not forget that these are simply the terms in which his work and life can be most easily translated. At a profound level, Brâncuşi is not contradictory. He shows a kind of consistency of spirit and esthetic that one might find in a rock. Brâncuşi's art is feminine. It is he, the sculptor, who is masculine. Brâncuşi the artist is the sole male in the world of his female forms. He sculpted few male forms: *Torso of a Young Man* (1917–22), *The Chief* (1924–25), *The King of Kings* (1938), *Adam* (who is part of *Adam and Eve*, 1916–21), *Narcissus Fountain* (1910–13), and *Plato* (which became *Little French Girl*, and then *Child*, thus feminizing itself), and *Socrates*. All these male forms are so philosophical as to be nearly androgynous. For the rest of it, Brâncuşi lived in a universe populated exclusively by the varied roundnesses of female forms.

Another apparent contradiction is that Brâncuşi, while demonstrably part of a time, a place, and an artistic spirit, also stands alone. I once said of William Blake, that he was a "jagged rock on the well-trimmed lawn of English literature." Something similar can be said of Brâncuşi who, like Blake, remains a visibly detached, awkwardly singular presence on the crowded boulevard of early twentieth-century art. He seems to be standing somehow above the shoulders of his contemporaries to gaze into an uncharted clarity. This gaze may very well be into the future where his shapes are already more comfortable but it can also be into the past, into the preliterate world of the Carpathian peasant who sits on a flat rock whittling an *ur*-bird.

In Brâncuşi these two worlds are simultaneous: he stands at the intersection of two forms of timelessness: one in which there is all the time in the world because time hasn't yet begun and one in which time has been expropriated by the machine. Romanian fairy tales often begin: "Once upon a time when there was no time, when time was an idea whose time hadn't come. . . ." In that time, a young girl, whose eyes had been stolen by a rival, turns into a bird. "God remembered her long waiting, her considered speech, her mild and unassuming manner and, when she finished her prayer, he turned her into a bird." Her feathers shone like "fireflies" and her eyes were human.

As for our now now, one can follow Brâncuşi's birds to tell the story of our time. I first saw his birds in pictures. I once had a dream about it. I dreamt that I was hiding the *Golden Bird* in a secret room. Two policemen came and dug up the whole garden in search of it. They found nothing and I was amused to think that policemen should be so stupid as to look for a bird in the ground. The whole time they were digging, the bird was there in the room but they couldn't see it because it had become "the invisible bird."

Looking at this bird, poised radiantly at the beginning of the twentieth century, Mina Loy, the great poet, wrote in 1922:

> *The toy*
> *become the esthetic archetype . . .*
> *This gong*
> *of polished hyperaesthesia shrills with brass*
> *as the aggressive light*
> *strikes*
> *its significance.*

Brâncuşi created in *The Bird* an enduring antidote of light to the coming darkness of police states and war. For seven decades Brâncuşi's hopelessly utopian bird in flight soared through the dimming lights of our century, looking terribly naive during the two world wars, only to charm us again when our souls were at rest. A few years ago, as I followed the collapse of the Red fascist dictatorship in Romania I kept seeing *The Magic Bird,* now rising, now eclipsed, now rising again. This bird became more than a sculpture, it shone, like Mina Loy said, with something archetypal, something we always had inside of us that simply took its place in our consciousness when Brâncuşi made it.

And then I saw the real thing. In a back room at the Chicago Art Institute the *Golden Bird* was being readied for exhibition. Having grown to mythic proportions in my mind I hadn't realized its quite modest dimensions. But that was, in fact, its secret. Rising there at an angle from its two pedestals, a wooden and a stone one, it elongated my hands and my face in its reflections, pulling me up with it. We soared together. Gravity be damned, it was okay to fly.

Brâncuşi said it himself: "Don't look for obscure formulas or mystery in my work. It is pure joy that I offer you. Look at my sculptures until you see them. Those closest to God have seen them."

So at the risk of simplicity, I'll say that Brâncuşi's sculpture brings one closer to God. Mircea Eliade, another mystical Romanian, once quoted Saint Sylvester thus: "God is like an onion because he is good and he makes you cry." Likewise, Brâncuşi is like an onion because he is good and he makes you fly.

Romanian and American Radio

I got a serious letter from a young scholar who proposes to compare and contrast Romanian and American radio. Not one to discourage young scholars, I offer the following, based on firsthand knowledge from when I was growing up.

Romanian radio was a wild preserve for folkloric ensembles that turned the nation's folklore into glue.

Romanian radio was the graveyard where old actors read ponderous poems by dead poets who turned in their graves, thus making the static that often accompanied these recitals.

Romanian radio assured me throughout my whole childhood that the five-year plan was being met in all the important areas, particularly in pig production and chemical fertilizers.

I could see that—just by looking around.

Romanian radio reserved its prime hours for the speeches of the dictator, which were so comforting the whole country fell asleep.

If Romanian radio were a drug it would be Sominex.

We pricked up our ears to Romanian radio only when the folk glue turned into a funeral march; then we knew that the boring leader who put us to sleep with his speeches had died.

When Gheorghiu-Dej, chief of the Communist Party died, everybody woke up for a minute.

He was followed shortly by the next sleeping pill, Nicolae Ceauşescu, whose own execution woke everybody up for a second.

The most memorable words ever uttered on Romanian radio were uttered on December 25, 1989, when the Ceauşescus were snuffed: "The Antichrist died on Christmas Day." Those were strong words, but soon after, the next sleeping pill, Ion Iliescu, started droning on.

In the evening, Romanian radio was tuned, throughout my childhood, to BBC, the Voice of America, and Radio Free Europe. People lowered their blinds and turned off their lights in the evening and stuck their ears to the radio. That's how we found out about the Beatles. If you walked down any street at night you could see the tiny radio lights informing people about the Beatles. As soon as I found out about the Beatles, I headed for America.

I didn't know that the Beatles lived in England—a good thing, or I might have ended up there, talking funny.

In America, the Beatles were on the radio.

Commercials were also on the radio.

American radio screamed where Romanian radio had whispered.

American radio screamed so many things I had to turn it off and still it came through the wall of the guy next door.

American radio didn't hide the news; it broadcast it twenty-four hours a day, which turned the world into glue.

American radio was the place where anybody could tell a bad joke.

American radio was like that in Detroit, but when I got to New York I heard WBAI and that was more like what I was looking for on the streets and in the music joints. It was more like the kind of sound I liked to hear in my life, not just on the radio.

American radio is not really American radio: it's a thousand kinds of radio. My kind of radio is smart radio with smart music, news that matters, analysis, and great ideas. That's NPR: they supply all that—music, news, and analysis—and I come up with the great ideas.

In Romania I lived outside the radio because I would have died of boredom if I'd gone inside it, but in America I live inside the radio, like a solid transistor, and entertain myself with all the little chips.

American radios are very big, especially in the cities. Sometimes they are as big as a truck and they can blow out your ears.

American radios can also be very small, hidden in a pencil or in eyeglasses.

Some people have radio coming out of their knees or their heads.

That's how much radio there is in America.

In Romania now the Beatles are on the radio.

And the commercials.

But Romanian radio is not American radio, even though there is more sound now. The glue goes on. And the bad poetry. And the pig quotas. And Sominex Iliescu.

But there is hope.

This is American-Romanian radio speaking.

World-Without-Walls:

The Impossible

Return

In the matter of walls, as in everything else, Henri Poincaré's maxim, "the scale is the phenomenon," holds—up to a point. The garden wall that Winston Churchill spent his retirement building for relaxation is not the Berlin Wall. The wall that Robert Frost claimed is wanted by "Something" can be construed as a mini–Berlin Wall, if one also adds Ted Berrigan's rejoinder, "I *am* that Something." The Great China Wall, Borges tells us, built by a mad emperor in order to stop history and to begin everything again starting with himself, is not the Maginot Line. Borges's China Wall is more a grand metaphor than a wall while the Maginot Line is more grand stupidity than wall. Some walls, like Borges's, are metaphorical, while others are merely symbolical. Others are just walls, as Freud might have said.

I grew up in an old medieval city with walled-in gardens and I truly loved walls. In front of my window was an ancient wall whose mosses and crenelations I knew by heart. My adolescent loneliness was identical to this wall. So was my desire to escape. The school I went to was an old fortified monastery with cannonballs still embedded in it, souvenirs of a sixteenth-century Turkish siege. The walls of my city were books. I could read them a little bit. Others could read them more. If my desire to escape hadn't been so strong I could have easily settled between the pages of the book of Sibiu, Transylvania, and made these walls my life reading.

The monks who once lived in my school had immured themselves here in order to defend their minds from the world. Outside my fortified city was the larger fortified province of Transylvania, made highly defensible by sheer mountains as well as by man-made walls. And outside Transylvania was the fortresslike country of Romania with its closely guarded borders, a country that was itself inside the larger prison of the Soviet system.

The literal walls that enclosed each of these entities were but the projections of history and systems, abstract walls that held against the battering rams of the outside world. To our keepers, those outside were barbarians even though, paradoxically, they were what even the jailers commonly called "Western civilization." In order to keep all these walls in place, our keepers went to great lengths to change the meanings of words. "Freedom" is what we had. "Slavery" is what those outside the walls wished for us. The desperate gymnastics of distortion, as Orwell has shown, were ubiquitous but unsteady. Often, we thought that by simply reversing them we would be free. But complexity and ambiguity shadowed ideology at every turn. All one had to do was look at the old walls, the abandoned fortifications, the defeated walled cities to know that all that industry had been in vain. As far as one would look the question of borders was there, even in myth.

There are two fundamental myths of the Romanian people: one very old, the other newer. The oldest posits the idea of border in harmony with the ecoregion and the cosmos. There are three brothers, shepherds. The youngest, who remains nameless, is told by his favorite sheep, Mioritza, who is also his confidante and lover, that he would be killed in the morning by his brothers. The young shepherd does not resist his fate. He spends the last night of his life by telling Mioritza to go to his mother and to tell her that he didn't really die, that he married the moon, and that all the stars had been at his wedding. In order to prepare Mioritza for his mother's questions, he describes each star at the wedding, its origin and its mission. By dawn he had described the entire cosmogony of the sky, all the origin myths of the stars. He is then killed and Mioritza wanders off telling his story, not just to his mother but to everyone who would listen. Mioritza wanders and wanders and is still wandering, telling his story. The path of her wanderings from the mountains to the sea is the natural border of Romania. In other words, this moving tale-telling border circumscribes the space of the Romanians. It is the path of the transmigration of sheep from mountains to sea, following the seasons.

Now, sometime in the Christian era, long after Mioritza's original journey, we hear about the Monastery of Argeş above the wild Argeş River. Three master craftsmen are building a church there on the rocky promontory overlooking the river. It is a high and highly defensible mountain fortress intended to stand forever. But the builders' labors are in vain. Every day the walls collapse. No amount of buttressing, reinforcing, or support can make them stand. One night, one of the builders dreams that the walls will not stand unless they build someone alive within them. The builders decide that the first of their wives to come with lunch the next day would be built into the monastery wall. They vow also not to tell their wives when they go home that night. But only the youngest builder, Master Manole, keeps his word. The other two tell their wives not to come. Master Manole's young and pretty wife shows up and she is slowly built into the wall by her heartbroken husband. She cries and asks why, and continues to cry and ask why even today, long after the church was built. The church still stands and the innocent victim still cries "Why?" But she can only be heard on certain nights, and few hear her.

Between these two myths stretches a quickening and a tightening, a vertiginous loss of liberty, the advent and conquest of prehistory by history. In prehistory the nomadic shepherds and their charges followed the cosmic rhythms of seasons and the topology of the land. But the older brothers' murder of the younger represents already a bid for history, a desire for surplus wealth beyond that allotted, an attempt to stop movement, to settle, to grow fat, to build walls. They are successful, but they are also thwarted by Mioritza, by the endlessly told story, which reinforces the ancient nomadic border and does not recognize the new borders of the fratricides.

These new borders will not, in fact, be established until the nomadic narrative is overthrown by another, by history proper, by chronicles written on the orders of kings, by chronology. Mioritza's narrative has been overthrown by the time of Master Builder Manole. History has firmly established its highly artificial and murderous boundaries, based on might, not geographical features. It is already clear that no great building (or city, state, or empire) will stand without the blood of the innocent. While Mioritza's shepherd still has recourse to a story that will avenge his death and retard history, the young wife of Master Manole has no such defense. She can only ask why. She has no story to leave behind, no narrative of the victim that will prevail over the injustice of her murder. The narratives of power, of murder, of surplus wealth, of mighty fortresses have become self-evident. The nomad, the woman, the young, the powerless, the victim, have been silenced. No one but the victim herself even bothers to ask why. It is obvious. The murderers' narrative has shut out the rhythms of nature.

The two victims, the young shepherd and Master Manole's wife are both nameless. They have already been buried in history. But while the young shepherd still has a voice, the voice of an animal, to tell his story, the young wife has only the wind to carry her question, and then only on certain nights. By the time of her murder, the animals have been silenced. They have become food, they have entered the slaughterhouse of production, they exist only for the benefit of the bloated conqueror-consumer. The only carrier of the world-without-walls is an enfeebled element, the wind. The elements still command a certain respect because their fury still escapes, occasionally, the wall-building abilities of man.

Since then, voices allied to the animals and the elements—the voices of artists, dreamers, children, the powerless, the voices of nature herself—have continued to ask an increasingly enfeebled "Why?" from under the cement bed of techno-civilization.

In yet other words, only an ecological perspective would let us out of the walls that currently define our space and, implicitly, out of the state of permanent war in which we live. If prior to the collapse of the Berlin Wall the illusion of two warring camps gave the militarization of the world a certain easily grasped rationale, no such excuse is available now. We are seeing, on the part of the military establishment, the desperate attempt to manufacture new threats of a smaller magnitude, which would keep them in business. Oil, religion, ethnic strife. Yet none of these have the grand moral authority of an adversary *system*.

Originally, I wanted to call this essay "ID'ing the Wallflower," because that's just how intrusive speech is. And then I felt the despair of psychology because the primary metaphor of "walls" in our time refers not to political freedom but to psychological defenses. Each one of us is a wall filled with tiny walls. Using that metaphor, one could address an audience only by the appellation "Distinguished Walls and Walls," because there is no way in English to distinguish the feminine and masculine of the word *wall*. The distinction may be clearer in a more discriminating tongue and I have no doubt that among the world's many vanished languages there was one that did just that. Those who wept by the waters of Babylon and are still weeping at the Wailing Wall may know exactly what gender the wall of their sorrow is. On the other hand, many languages have doubtlessly disappeared precisely when they became too discriminating on the matter of walls. That is to say, the people who spoke them disappeared and the languages with them. At the point when they achieved a degree of sophistication that made plain the notion of gender-specific walls, the barbarians came from the hills and wiped out everyone with the sounds ugh! ugh! And I'm for the barbarians, you understand.

But to continue on this slippery slope: since the neolithic, women have been given the world between walls (or in the walls) while men have been charged with building and defending them. I say "since the neolithic" because that's a little before Mioritza's time, when hunting-gathering was a group affair, and building unknown. The neolithic cave did not have walls. In the postneolithic the genders divided the upkeep of buildings: women became keepers of the interior while men patrolled the outside. Since there is a lot more outside than there is inside, men would seem to have more freedom while women would seem to become prisoners. I say "seem," because such constructs are tenuous. The men's so-called freedom was the slavery of wall-building while the women's so-called slavery contained the freedom of time, available only in a cell. What we now call the war between the sexes is a war over space or if you like over freedom. Prisoners develop extensions of freedom that are inconceivable to free people. One of these extensions is language.

Women invented language in order to restructure the world more equitably given the fact that the outside was occupied by men. Women wove stories out of language that made the outside-inside distinctions tenuous. In this way, they invented psychology. The existence of inner space is a late postneolithic development that served the purpose of freeing women and imprisoning men. When psychology became indivisible from language, the tribe experienced delirium, ecstasy, transcendence. Then the barbarians came, ugh! ugh!

The only creature worthy of respect is the wallflower. A creature is a wall. Respect is space. Therefore, worth is the space one accords a wall. Some walls are:

1. The Great Wall of China, said, erroneously, I think, to be visible from space (our space mythology allows only for *one* wall since, clearly, space is the very lack of walls except as "respect," i.e., metaphorically); the China wall is now a tourist wall, used to keep out metaphorical barbarians.
2. The Berlin Wall, which was once a real wall plus a metaphor, but it's now only a metaphor plus a few commodified chunks.
3. A prison wall (mostly real though it extends metaphorically way beyond its actual dimensions).
4. Roman walls all over Europe that are mostly wall parts but are curiously devoid of metaphor.
5. Wal-Mart, sorry, that's not a wall, it's a *world*.
6. A wall left standing after a bomb (just a wall, symbolic or not).

If you hand a poet the word *wall* he will wall you in language.

If you put a poet (like a harem girl) between walls she will wail until you let her out.

The prison house of language has served to imprison people, but it's only poets who take it apart brick by brick.

The Victorian home was made to keep women intra-*murus*.

Psychology is rearranging the furniture (perhaps breaking down some walls) in the prison house of language in the house of a shrink who has invested *mucho* in his walls.

Prison planet: gravity is a wall.

The church will not stand if you don't build a girl into the wall.

Name the people disappeared behind walls lately.

What walls story themselves with the bodies they contain?

One wall talking to another: "The one lying right there with the one eye the life etc." Plaster verbs.

To speak of walls is to speak of nothing less than the fundamental project of civilization, as opposed to nature. To be asked to speak of walls is then either the expression of an unlimited faith in the *nature* of expression or a plea for an ecological defense of the primitive world, a defense using language merely to point to the survival of a world without walls. Or, to be more realistic, to the idea of it since the existence of such a world outside utopia is accessible now only by nonrational, nonlinguistic means. The world without walls is defending itself by making itself unavailable to language even as we continue to deplete its energies.

Fifteen years ago I wrote a poem called "Politics":

> *you are in a barbed land and you are NOT dying.*
> *the claws of the grass are bent*
> *inwards. likewise the trees are tearing nothing*
> *but their own hearts. everything holds in*
> *the bleeding meat of self-injury.*
> *surrounded by protection from each other*
> *we have left the inside*
> *vulnerable.*
> *it is the walls i hate with all my heart*
> *and those who, dead inside,*
> *have built them from their own disfigured corpses.*

Politics. Fifteen years ago the barbed wire atop the walls between my native country and the West was literally still there. Yet this was not the politics I was concerned with: the land of which I was speaking was barbed, yet one did not die there. This walled-in world was internal as well as external and it was situated in a psychological landscape. What is more, nature too had become internalized by the malignant extention of political consciousness. The clawed grass and the bent trees were deformed by the peculiar fear that drives human organization. I felt hemmed in by the spiritually dead conformists whose corpses piled up in every direction, making the horizon—as well as liberty—unreachable. But if *I* felt that way, I could only lament—not imagine—the sorrow of a nature thus confined.

The walls erected against the imagination in our time are both more substantial and more durable than their counterparts in the so-called real world because they are built from within by the accumulated debris of one's own life. Under these conditions, the very existence of a universe outside of ourselves comes under question. The violently humanized universe leaves only traces of its former infinity.

To speak of walls is to speak first of all of the splendor and horror of liberty and its multiple opposites. From such splendor and horror are born the forms of the *socius:* the tribe, the nation, and the family, organized, all of them, for the purposes of keeping out the Outside, that wild, cosmic, self-selecting Outside from which we humans have been subtracting ourselves, if such a thing were possible. It's on that *if* a certain hope rests.

To survey even part of this multi-tentacled diminishment of the consciousness of the universe, one needs to strap on one's sturdiest pair of wings and swoop down on language where all that has ever been constructed has found its arena of ambiguous translation. Suffice it to say that the walls of Jericho will crumble only when we are speechless before our final destruction. All the rest is language. Words themselves are walls. (As I write this the walls of Jericho surface in the news. It looks now that they might not crumble after all or that they may crumble happily and we'll survive them, but it's too soon to tell.)

All modes of human habitation can be described by the shape and position of their walls. The defenses of tribes, the self-defenses of individuals, the megalomaniacal projects of dictators. Only after that, and at a markedly more pedestrian level, does one look at real walls and their symbolic projections. In their historic extensions walls are strictly a matter of scale.

The stark concrete matter that was once the Berlin Wall was exhibited all over the world after 1989, like the traveling fragments of "the true cross" in the Middle Ages. The chunks were loaded with symbolism intended to represent the division of the world into two warring camps, or at least a certain view of the world that conceived of it in that way. But the Iron Curtain of which the Berlin Wall was the visible translation had pretty much ceased to exist by the midsixties. For my generation, growing up behind the Iron Curtain in those days, Communist ideology had ceased to exist, if it ever did exist for us. We felt that we had much more in common with our contemporaries in the West, and that our common enemy, East and West, was not ideology but the old people who clung to its outmoded languages. In truth, the Hair Curtain that fell between generations was vastly more significant to us than the carefully maintained fantasies of cold warriors on both sides. In the Prague Spring of 1968 our sentiments received a crude shock from the old men of the Soviet military establishment, just as the youth of the West received its own correction from the police and the National Guard in Paris and Chicago. The crumbling ideologies managed to hold on to their wall through the use of brute power for nearly two more decades.

When the Berlin Wall finally came down, the meaning of its collapse was more than ambiguous. Of course, for a little less than ten minutes there was no ambiguity. In the euphoria of the actual physical event, it was generally believed that freedom had come to the so-called Soviet empire and that the people of those regions could now aspire to Western standards of prosperity, which would be brought about by the so-called free market, with attendant democracy.

This is not quite what happened. The Berlin Wall, like a mythical dragon, spawned a thousand little walls that are growing as we speak. First of all, the released inmates of the ex-Soviet zone were startled to find themselves unwelcome to the other side of the Wall. Their unrealistic expectations of prosperity were quickly quashed when American airplanes full of everything advertised on TV since 1953 failed to show up. The cargo cult that sprang up in 1989 soon gave way to a disappointed nationalism. On the Western side of the Wall, the sudden appearance of real people from behind the veil of ideology caused a panic that blossomed quickly into xenophobic nationalism. Nationalism is the ideology of the tribal wall. The inner side of this wall is constructed of the sentimental kitsch of a dubious history while the outer bristles with implacable hate for the neighboring nationals, busy building their own wall. The history of the recent past is the history of the hasty erection of a variety of walls to contain the breach of the Berlin Wall.

Nowhere is this more evident than in Germany, where the cost of reunification has already caused plenty of doubt as to the wisdom of it. The rebirth of German nationalism under conditions of unemployment and hatred of foreigners is strong déjà vu. At the beginning of 1993 Germany deported back to Eastern Europe hundreds of thousands of immigrants, mostly Gypsies, by making cash deals with governments such as Romania where the returning deportees were sure to face persecution. No one would dream in 1989 that the words *Germany, Gypsies,* and *deportation* could be used in the same sentence again. The unknown

Holocaust, as it has been called, of Gypsies at the hands of Germans in World War II has been nearly forgotten. Gypsies, like the Jews, were marked for extermination by the Germans, who deported them to concentration camps in the East. Today, the German government does not use cattle wagons but deutsche marks to deport its undesirables. One further irony, worthy of note: in the mid-1960s Germany bought freedom for German speakers in Romania by paying as much as $4,000 a person to the Communist government. Today, it is paying considerably less to throw non-Germans out of its territory. The price of freedom is, apparently, set by something other than democratic ideals.

Let us see what other freedoms were unleashed by the destruction of the Berlin Wall. The freedom to travel was once a much sought-after privilege by the citizens of the Red zone. The prohibitive cost of such desire in the post-totalitarian economies has made such freedom merely theoretical. One can argue, as the Germans, other Europeans, and Americans do, that these peoples' desire to travel is merely a disguise for running away from their countries. Visas have thus become more difficult to obtain and the obstacle to freedom of travel comes now, ironically, from Western countries. Before 1989, travel within the disappeared empire was fairly uncomplicated. But try to travel now between Belgrade and Sarajevo, for instance, or between Moscow and Tbilisi. Walls? Ideology? We gots plenty.

And let's take freedom of speech, another cherished notion of pre-1989, which rallied the intellectuals of the world. Today, in Romania, to take a single country, though it's true about all the others, anyone is free to say anything. And Anyone does. Anyone has been speaking— torrents of speech, rivers of language. The vulgate has been unleashed in a din that makes rock 'n' roll sound like chamber music. Pornography, astrology, fascist propaganda, scandal gossip, all the freedoms of speech that have so effectively narcotized us here in the West, have flooded the hitherto silent zones. The *littérateurs* who have been the very ones to call for freedom of speech are now lamenting the fact that no one reads them any longer. Many of them have become shockingly aware of the irony of their position: they have been the very instruments of their own obsolescence. Their power, which had been extraordinary in the days of censorship, has borne a variety of philosophical fruit, some of which has been distinctly poisonous. Take the concept of Central Europe, advanced by Konrad and Kundera, among others. This mythic Central Europe that looked nostalgically back to the Austro-Hungarian Empire has now *become* the Austro-Hungarian—or perhaps the German—Empire, with all the attendant nationalist tensions of that entity. Left out of Central Europe, on the other side of an invisible wall of so-called western culture, are countries like Romania, Bulgaria, and Russia. But it is clear now that decades of Red fascism have caused the same human and cultural problems in *all* the countries under Soviet control, regardless of their position on the map or their history. The fiction of Central Europe is hardly maintainable in these circumstances.

One can go on piling up ironies by degrees of bitterness. The so-called market reforms, including the right to private property are in the hands of former party apparatchiks turned entrepreneurs or gangsters, the distinction is often hard to make. The word *democracy*, once used to great effect to criticize the authoritarian Communist Party is being openly manipulated by those same people to cynically accumulate power and to steal more brazenly than ever. Even the secret police have been "privatized" and are doing a bang-up business in files and secrets, as well as in ordinary thuggery, forgery, assassination, and whatever else may be in demand.

So, was it better before? one might ask. The answer to that question is that there was no before before, not for a long time. By 1989 it was clear to everyone—with the possible exception of the CIA—that the Soviet Byzantium was rotten to the core. It had been rotten since 1968, as Gorbachev himself admitted, and the only reason it was still being tolerated was that people's so-called freedoms were irrelevant to the world economic system, were, in fact, a bother to it. In debt up to their necks to Western banks, the Soviets and their puppets had to be maintained so that they could pay. When it became obvious that they couldn't either pay *or* be maintained, the West did what any financial institution would do: declared the whole enterprise bankrupt and moved to auction off the physical plant. There couldn't be anyone naive enough to think that any ideology, except that of commerce, was still operating by 1989. And where did that leave the people, the long-suffering people of the faux Red empire?

It left them shattered by their own burst of optimism, which is to say in the same place where they had been consigned innumerable times by a less than propitious history. Under these circumstances, nationalism is a major allergic reaction to powerlessness. Its suicidal virulence does draw attention, however.

An argument against such reading is made these days using the mystical notion of transition. Yes, it's true, the remaining optimists (mostly Westerners, incidentally) will tell you, these countries are in bad shape but it's only a transition. The advocates of transition, a phenomenon said to last anywhere between one and three generations, will tell you that eventually Eastern Europe will be absorbed into a unified Europe, and that Europe itself will be part of the United Nations of the World. Another utopia at hand! The world without walls. The notion of transition resembles more than anything the notion of Purgatory, introduced in the Middle Ages by the Church in order to do business in indulgences and forgiveness. Everyone gets to heaven eventually if they pay the price. The length of one's stay in Purgatory varies according to one's ability to sacrifice. Well, the nationalists are ready to sacrifice everything: they want to go to Hell or to Heaven, whichever comes first, in a burst of fire. Therapeutic *Götterdämmerung*.

Where Have All the Jokes in Eastern Europe Gone?

The history of the last forty years in Eastern Europe, from Marxism to Groucho-Marxism, can be told in jokes. It is an extremely primitive history, almost a non-history, resembling a simple organism with about three bones. It is quite amazing, given such history's lack of complexity, that armies of Western experts spent decades sifting with lice combs through Politburo speeches and opiated economic reports. They could have saved a heap of time if they had known that Khrushchev left three unopened envelopes for his successors. Inside the first was written, "Relax censorship. Declare amnesty. When this stops working, open the second envelope." In the second envelope it said, "Borrow from the capitalists. Close your eyes to the black market. When this stops working, open the third envelope."

Inside the third envelope was this: "Write three messages for your successor. Seal the envelopes."

At the height of the Stalinist terror, at the political joke contest, there were three prizes: third prize, a hundred rubles; second prize, two hundred rubles; first prize, ten years at hard labor. This political joke contest was the same everywhere in the ex-Soviet dystopia with few local variations. In that sense, the equalitarian ideal was first realized not on the economic or social level but in the amusement zone. The universality of the political joke achieved what the serious ideologues could only dream of: the universal recognition of a common *something*. That "something" turned out to be misery. During Stalinism a joke could have swift consequences: the release of the punchline was followed by the incarceration of the punster. Every joke during those days had, in effect, only one punchline: the Gulag. I have no firsthand knowledge of anyone incarcerated for a joke because I was only old enough to go to prison during the time punsters were amnestied, but the experience must have made instant philosophers out of the victims. The Gulag must have contained thousands of Kierkegaards. The universal content of the ex-Soviet political joke did not diminish after the end of Stalinism, but the distribution improved as the punishments lessened. By the midsixties the secret police became a kind of center for the dissemination of jokes: they avidly collected and spread them. It became evident after Khrushchev de-Stalinized the political waters that jokes had no authors. You couldn't imprison someone for having an antenna. A single source for such jokes could not be found: the political jokes were the creation of the collective mind, spontaneous as wind-borne spores, everywhere and nowhere at once. On the surface of the still waters of state socialism the jokes bred like mosquitoes, taking off in swarms to keep the overheated bureaucrats awake at siesta time.

By the mid-1960s life itself became a joke in Eastern Europe, or, at least, there was no other modality to express it. The Joke became the quintessential form of truth-telling, and it had to be capitalized, as Milan Kundera finally did in the novel *The Joke*. In addition to the joke's time-honored parabolic, satirical, and pedagogical functions, there was an added existential-eschatological dimension that included everything. The Joke metamorphosed to become total. The inhabitants of the interior of the Joke reflected it in myriads of ways. They laughed to death, and others laughed and died watching them. Laughter became a rictus that disfigured the faces of the citizenry as it lived, wallowed, and died in the Joke. By 1968, the state itself was the chief producer of a generalized Joke that held the place previously reserved for the sentimental platitudes of ideology. Stalinism had attempted—and failed—to oppose heroic, romantic, socialist-realist sentiments to jokes.

But it failed only with adults. While fear made grown-ups pretend to be impressed by utopian verbal and granite statuary, children were *truly* impressed. The Young Pioneers, to which I belonged, were the only ones capable of envisioning a nonjocular existence and, say what they will, we were irrevocably awed by the sentimental monumenology of Stalinism. It impressed itself on our souls. A Stalinist core of seriousness was planted in us at an age when we were full of generalized faith. I remember standing bare-kneed in the dewy morning of our pioneer camp with my hand to my temple, promising, "In the name of Marx, Engels, Lenin, Stalin, and Gheorghiu-Dej, forward!," a tongue twister that left some of the verbally impaired gasping for air. In that rarefied air from which most of our fathers had vanished to labor camps we could behold the face of Stalin, our true and only father, his kind mustaches dipping downward to nestle us between their comforting parentheses. By the time Stalin died it was too late for us to be de-Stalinized. A tiny Stalin waved his arms in a tiny amphitheater built specifically for him in our hearts.

In the years to come, our consequent disappointment was the result of an internal argument with the facts of daily life that bashed themselves with waving arms against this utopian rock. The Joke of life in the sixties was fiercer and more grotesque for the resistance it encountered as it battered itself against our Young Pioneer hearts.

Kundera's novel *The Joke* follows the Joke in one of its most familiar guises: simulation of the real. Everything in his midsixties Prague is a simulation. Folkloric "ensembles" imitate folklore. Communist Party members imitate Western capitalist fashions. Young Czech kids imitate what they imagine to be young American kids. Imitation extends to emotional life where everyone is caught in a whirl of simulation of feelings. The lies have become so generalized it is impossible to remember the truth. The truth, of course, has been relativized by earlier imitations and is now without expression.

In Romania, the Joke, under Ceauşescu, didn't become total because his brand of national socialism, while kitsch in the extreme, actually seduced both some people who knew better, and the idiot masses which, not necessarily idiotic in small numbers, become rhinocerized *en masse*. In small numbers, Romanians have a wicked, self-deprecating humor that is full of common sense, even in ethnic jokes. When Itzak and

Shmuel decide to escape from Romania by covering themselves with a cow skin and pretending to be a cow peacefully grazing at the border, it is not the border guards that get them. Itzak spying from underneath the tail screams in terror. "The border guards?" shouts Shmuel. "No, stupid! The bull!"

So—Romanians do not question anybody's desire to leave. Nor do they have much respect for the police. But the bull, that's another story! Toro, the bull, Mithra, is the spirit of the land incarnate. You can defy temporal authority, but watch out for this bull! The Ceauşescu brand of nationalism did what it could to incite this unquestionable and aroused national bull to attack the minorities living in the country. Jews, Gypsies, Hungarians, Germans, all were under the shadow of this horny bull. When at last, after Ceauşescu's downfall, this bull escaped its Joke, there was nothing funny about it.

The kitsch of Czech folkloric assemblages was not entirely jocular for us because the Romanian nationalist bull was still real to many people of the prewar generation. Romanian fascism, while crude like all the rest of fascisms, was more green than brown, and the smell of bull was strong and unfunny. That is, there was an added unfunniness to the basic unfunniness of fascism, which is axiomatically suicidal and thus incapable of bearing the paradox of suffering with either grace or humor. The suicided fascists of Romania were encouraged throughout the seventies and eighties to resurface their deadly brown myths. It is this brown, an ecological longing really, that seduced some of the younger generation in the Ceauşescu era. The mutterings of the pious cadaver of national fascism found some willing receptors in the smothered utopian cores of our Young Pioneers. We had taken our oaths in the woods, but the woods were quickly being smothered by industry. The idealized peasant life was being destroyed by rapid industrialization. It is not surprising that one of the first new political parties formed after 1989 was the Romanian Ecological Party, and it is not surprising that after a brief period of resembling its Western counterparts, the Romanian Ecological Party made an alliance with the right-wing nationalists. Their slogan, "A clean man in a clean country in a clean world," was ready-made for that merging. So much cleanliness gave me the creeps right from the start. "Ethnic cleansing" wasn't far behind. The deconstruction of jokes began under the nationalist policies of Ceauşescu. Their disappearance in post-Communism is the end of that process.

For Kundera the real and the real-sounding were complete and perfect opposites. He believed that a discerning, or merely awake, person would be capable of telling the difference, though he acknowledged that it was a difficult operation. In the capitalist West, where imitations are done in plastic, the job of telling them apart has already become impossible. But in the East, where the technology of propaganda was still based on crude, slow, and laborious substitutions, an intelligent person could, at times, intuit the genuine. One means to express such intuition was to have a knack for metaphors that matter. Kundera's "laughter and forgetting," "lightness and heaviness" are of this order. Using "laughter and forgetting," Kundera was able to create a phenomenal critique of memory that held within it, amazingly, the potential for a certain sobriety, and for the more ambitious, the possibility of mnemonic demiurgy. He pointed to the exact place in his own memory where the real was replaced by the simulacrum, which was also the place where the generative, creative urge is located. This is also the place where jokes originate. The paradox of remembering and inventing, being located at the same place, is a nifty one, probably unavailable to most people, who use memory as a springboard for murderous indignation rather than an occasion for improvisation. Nonetheless, people had jokes to sustain them in paradox. Without jokes it will not be possible for most people to live in the new post-Communist Europe which, so far, has shown us only the grim face of its outraged memory. Without a handy imaginative mnemo-erogeny, or a good joke, there is little hope.

Having come to artistic maturity about the time of the Prague Spring in 1968, and then gone into exile in the 1970s, Kundera had to remake himself in order to continue. In order to write he had to remember, but in order to be he had to forget. What to forget and what to remember? It is a tension peculiar to exile, but it is also a common human predicament. In the West, where we are faced with the catastrophic loss of memory brought about by industreality, we are daily compelled to forget even the immediate past by the collage style of the mass media. Living in a continual forgetting (an active act), we can only face forward, in a kind of parody of the Communist goal, which always bids the masses to step "forward." Progress is the act of forgetting. In the East, where progress was the state god, history was rewritten to fit its heroic and jocular demands, so remembering was a point of honor. How Eastern Europeans remember turns out to be the crucial means of understanding them now. But what is the point (and indeed, the strength) of that honor when the honorable person doesn't live in the familiar Communist Joke anymore, but in a postmodern Elsewhere where forgetting is such sweet narcotic?

This is a question that has to be considered in light of recent events.

"Is it true," a reporter asks Ceauşescu in the spring of 1989, "that your people are freezing from lack of heat?" "Yes," Ceauşescu replies, "but nobody died from that." "Is it true," insists the reporter, "that there is no food and everyone is starving?" "It is true," Ceauşescu says, "but nobody ever died from it." The astonished interviewer throws up his hands. "Have you tried cyanide?" he asks.

Next to Ceauşescu himself, his wife, Elena, was the most hated person in the country. It appears that, at long last, a citizen obtained a gun and tried to kill the dictator at a mass rally. But he missed. "How could you possibly miss?" asks the colonel in charge of torturing him. "It was the crowd," the man says, "they kept shoving me this and that way: shoot him, shoot her. . . ."

These were possibly the last jokes told about the Ceauşescus. It was as if even the jokes had run out of anything but the crude fantasy of revenge. In the end, Ceauşescu did try cyanide on his own people—his security forces were said to have poisoned the water in Sibiu—and he would have taken the country with him if he'd been able to occupy the country's only nuclear plant. And the citizen-assassin, who in November, had been only a character in a joke, became only too real in December when he and his friends pumped a great number of bullets into the tyrants' bodies.

Today, the Ceauşescus' grave site is a place of pilgrimage. People leave flowers on it every day and claim, without a trace of irony, that things were much better when the tyrants were in charge. These people undoubtedly told Ceauşescus jokes before their deaths. What they are lamenting is not really the Ceauşescus, but the disappearance of the jokes that made their own lives bearable. They are laying flowers on the grave of the Joke.

If political jokes were once cartoons derived from reality, they have now become grimly real. But they are not jokes anymore. Life in Eastern Europe is still a joke but, paradoxically, it is a joke without humor. The pun was replaced by the gun.

The editor of a Romanian humor magazine, Mr. Ioan Morar, came to visit me in New Orleans around Mardi Gras. I asked him what happened to all the jokes that people used to tell before the fall of Communism. Before 1989 people used to live on jokes. There wasn't anything else. Now people scream, swear, weep over stupid nationalist songs, and beat each other up. They don't tell jokes.

Mr. Morar said that it was true, jokes had disappeared, but that Romanians had other venues for political humor now: satirical-political magazines like his own, stand-up comics and musical-comedic revues that played to sold-out crowds.

I pointed out that these things were okay, but that they were rather highbrow affairs, while jokes are for everyone. I kept thinking about this phenomenon later, while we watched a Mardi Gras parade. Mr. Morar enjoyed the carnival immensely: he jumped up and down like a kid when floats went by. But when the navy bands and the ROTC drill teams appeared, he drew back with a worried expression on his face. I reassured him that these military types were not out to harm us. Some of them, in fact, had beads and feathers on their rifles. I don't know if my explanation satisfied him, but I had an inkling about why there may be no more jokes in Eastern Europe. On the one hand, everybody still jumps up and down about being rid of tyrants. On the other, the uniforms keep marching by. At least, during the familiar misery of the past, the rifles were within constant view. But this odd alternation of clowns and rifles, exaltation and anxiety, this is too unsettling for jokes. Jokes need stability.

It is said that if you are Romanian, you can be born either in a city or in the country. If you are born in the city, that's fine. If you are born in the country, there are two possibilities: you can stay home and die of hunger or you can enlist in the army. If you stay home and die of hunger, that's fine. If you enlist in the army, there are two possibilities. You can get a job behind a desk or you could be sent to the front. If you get a desk job, that's fine. If you get sent to the front, there are two possibilities. You could be wounded or you could be killed. If you get wounded, that's fine. If you get killed, there are two possibilities. You could be thrown in a common grave, or you could get your own. If you get your own, that's fine. If you get thrown in a common grave, there are two possibilities: a tree will grow out of you, or nothing will. If a tree grows out of you, that's fine. If nothing grows—etc.

People told this joke waiting in line for food during the dictatorship. The idea was to see how many possibilities you could discover until you got to the front of the line. There was usually nothing when you got there, but that was distinctly one of the possibilities. Of course, death meant nothing to the realm of possibilities, and Romanians, in particular, have highly developed myths to deal with the contingency of death. The breadline had another function in my day. My mother used to wake me up at five in the morning to go stand in the line. When I got back, she didn't ask me first whether I got the bread or the milk. She asked me what I'd heard in the line. That line was our true newspaper: that's where we heard the gossip, the rumors, and the jokes. The food was secondary in importance to the telegraph that broadcast the real news of our community.

Today, the lines are still long if not longer. But the kind of news that used to feed us can be found in the newspapers. The jokes have given way to what they had been containing all along: anger at the continuing misery. Jokes used to find their culprits in the absurd gap between ideology and some kind of decency. Today's culprits are not to be found in the absurdities of the ideology but rather in the archetypal scapegoats of the pre-Communist era: Jews, Gypsies, Americans, foreign capital, speculators, etc. Salvation, once thought possible only through Western intervention, has now returned to its proper mystical ground, and found its language on the moldering wallpaper of nationalist poetry.

Forty years of poverty and corruption were unable to create enough material objects to begin the process of forgetting. After forty years of eating jokes, people were ready for something better. When they didn't get it, they stripped their jokes of humor and turned them into weapons. The racial stereotypes in jokes became real. When emotionally depleted people are suddenly disappointed and further starved, they revert to whatever is singularly theirs in recent memory, in this case bloody folk songs and calls for revenge.

Jokes belong to a more benign era.

Sigmund **Freud** in **Romania**

It has been argued, and I agree, that Eastern Europe and what used to be the Soviet Union need a psychiatrist before anything else, including democracy and market reform. And not just any psychiatrist, but Sigmund Freud himself. Now, a small foundation, the Romanian Foundation for the Translation of Sigmund Freud, has set out to provide just that.

The RFTSF is embarked on an ambitious program to bestow psychoanalysis to a place where the mere mention of the master's name was forbidden for forty years. The Communists would not allow psychoanalysis to be taught because they believed that the ills of individuals are to be found in bourgeois society and that socialist man had no such traumas. Well, it turns out they were right. Communist societies so trau-

matized human beings one wishes they had only simple, bourgeois up-
bringing to blame for rampant psychosis. Given the recent elections of
former Communists and born-again fascists it would seem that psychoanalysis is too mild a treatment, shock therapy being more appro-
priate.

But there is one distinct advantage to Freudian analysis, namely the
telling of stories. The people of those countries badly need to tell their
stories. They need to lie down on the couch of their history and let the
stories of their injuries flow. The shock of passing from a closely patrolled police state to relative freedom of expression has rendered people practically catatonic. The fear of opening up their impoverished and
dark worlds accounts for their opting to return to the safety of their recent sickness. Translating Freud may help.

On the other hand, who is going to play psychoanalyst when everyone traumatized by the system is sick? That job would fall to us in the
West, not that we are so sane ourselves. Still, if we knew how to listen,
it would be worth as much as banking credits and high-flown rhetoric
about "democracy." I'm afraid, though, that we do not know how—nor
do we want—to listen. The pain of that recently shattered world leaves
us cold. But if we repress it, as Freud suggests, we may be nurturing
worse demons.

Pain News

To seemingly unrelated stories from Eastern Europe point to a new situation over there. The first is that Dracula's Bran Castle in Transylvania, Romania, needs $300,000 worth of repairs or it's going to fall down. "If we have an earthquake or if something is not done, it will just fall down," Cornel Talos, the castle's architectural director, said.

The other bit of news is that city authorities in Lvov, Ukraine, have been tormenting a group of artists who want to honor Leopold von Sacher-Masoch, the famous masochist, who was born in their city in 1836. The artists have formed an International Masoch Fund and are trying to persuade the U.N. to declare 1995 "the Year of Masoch." The Lvov city council has been rejecting the pleas of the Ukrainian Masochophiles.

The international community, which has been indifferent to so many of the problems of post-Communist Eastern Europe, such as hunger, economic development, and the rise of nationalism, can no longer afford to remain on the sidelines. If Dracula ends up having no place to live he might just move to the West permanently. Our immigration problems being what they are, I don't think we can handle it.

Leopold Masoch, on the other hand, has much to offer the West. The twentieth century has had more sufferers than just about any other, and none of them have suffered voluntarily. Masoch offers us the possibility of suffering pleasurably by laying down the terms of our contract of pain. Masoch is a lawyerly lens through which we can transform our pains into ecstasies. He is very much like Christ, only more bureaucratic.

These two indispensable, symbolic pillars of our pained and painful world, Dracula and Masoch, are in danger. Let's help them get together in a renovated castle. We need them, they need each other, I need a vacation.

Where Is the **Heart** of Transylvania?

I am fond of American Unitarians. It's the only church I don't feel like running screaming out of. The Unitarian Church I have experienced—as a guest, not a member—seems to me a happy place, a community-oriented organization based on acceptance, tolerance, and inclusion. In Louisiana I know atheists, Jews, and socialists who go to Unitarian meetings to hear intelligent discussions of their community. The emphasis seems to me to be on love and tolerance, not on fearful injunctions from life.

I have always known that something called the Unitarian Church had its origin in Transylvania, where I was born. Near my grandmother's home town, Alba Iulia, is a beautiful old church. When I was a child I liked to sneak into the courtyard and lie unseen on the hot stones near the central fountain. It was a peaceful and magical place.

Unitarianism was established in the mid-sixteenth century and was proclaimed, for a brief time, the official religion of Transylvania by King John Sigismund. It was a remarkable achievement at a time when life must have seemed pretty uncertain. The wars with the Turks were more or less constant. The quarrels of nobles with each other and with their princes transformed every region into a maze of divided loyalties and complex allegiances. The doctrines of Dr. Martinus Luther had gained followers very quickly among the merchant class in the German-speaking areas, as well as in Hungary and Poland. The Reformation, as Luther's movement came to be called, threatened the privileges of the Catholic clergy, fattened by influence, wealth, and the selling of indulgences. The distressed Hapsburgs launched a campaign known as the Counter-Reformation against the followers of Luther. The Counter-Reformation began competing with the Reformation to make the church hipper, more up-to-date, and jazzier, believing that the popular appeal of the Reformation lay in its accessibility. Of course, this was only part of the competition, which included, among other things, the burning of witches, practiced by both Lutherans and Catholics with increasing frequency. While the Catholics had accommodated women in the church through the cult of Mary, the younger division had not yet given women much room to breathe and given Luther's misogyny, it wasn't going to for a long time. Neither church had much use for the Jews. Luther was a notorious anti-Semite, the true father of the modern European anti-Semitism that gave us the Holocaust.

The mid-sixteenth century is called by scholars "the premodern age," because, on the one hand, it was neither as creative as the Renaissance nor yet as positive as the modern age. The chief difference between the Reformation and the Counter-Reformation was that the Reformers did not believe in the imminent end of the world. The medieval church had become mired in the mud of eschatology and all its business got tied up in the afterlife. Hence, the selling of indulgences.

Far from ending, the world was, in fact, experiencing a new beginning. The discovery of the Americas promised incomparable wealth and abundance to the Europeans. The horizons of the limited medieval world expanded suddenly outside the imagination with the advent of far-reaching exploration. The nobility, whose tenuous hold on absolute power had been weakening, made grudging room for the new merchant class and had to admit the existence of the lower classes. The newly enfranchised, whether the nouveaux riches or the freedom-hungry artisans, and even the peasants, wanted a bigger piece of God. A more intelligible and useful piece of God, you might say. Luther provided this by offering the Bible in the vernacular. In doing this, he bypassed the bureaucracy-heavy machinery of the Catholic Church, which had grown into an unwieldy and grotesque organism.

The changes wrought by the Reformation benefited the kings and princes as well, who seized the opportunity to strengthen central power against the perennial destabilizing claims of the nobles. This is the time when Niccolò Machiavelli's *Prince* made its impact in the real world. The modern state was born at this time. Unlike the weak medieval state, the modern state was based on central power and on criteria other than the kinship of ancient families. These new criteria were religion and nationality.

In 1566, the Reformed Church was still in a state of flux. Its doctrines had not yet become fixed. But it was already clear to John Sigismund, prince of the independent principality of Transylvania, that the success of his rule depended on the coexistence of several religious points of view. Transylvania was, even in those times, the quintessential multicultural region. The Hungarian nobles, who were for the most part Catholic, ruled a population of Protestant Hungarian and Saxon tradesmen, and Orthodox Romanian peasants. The region was inhabited by Hungarians, Romanians, Saxons, Székelys, and some Jews. The Székelys, made famous by the descriptions of Bram Stoker at the beginning of his gothic masterpiece, *Dracula,* were a fierce tribe from Asia who had been imported to guard the borders of Transylvania against the relentless attacks of the Turks.

To further complicate matters, Transylvania, while nominally independent, was in fact a vassal of the Turks, to whom it paid yearly tribute. The lower principalities of Romania, as well as Hungary, were also vassals of the Turks. What this meant was that they were not officially included within the borders of the Turkish empire, but were in a subservient position nevertheless. The Turks, despite their invocation of Allah before battle, were relatively tolerant of the religious beliefs of people within their sphere of influence. This was partly realpolitik. They realized that it would have been impossible forcibly to convert millions of believers. But it was also tolerance, a virtue that has been part of moderate Islam since its founding.

John Sigismund ruled over an unstable gumbo of potentially destructive forces. He convened the first debate on religions in 1566 in my grandmother's town of Alba Iulia, known as Gyulafehérvár in Hungarian. This city in Transylvania is of great importance to all the people living there. It is a sacred locus for the Romanians whose ancestors, the Dacians, had their capital of Sarmisegetuza there, before their conquest by the Romans. The ceremonies of Romania's coronations and that of the unification of Transylvania with Romania have taken place here. By the time Sigismund convened the religious leaders, the town had already had a long and distinguished history.

This meeting attempted to resolve the question of which religion should become the official state religion of Transylvania. Three branches of the Reform Church vied for attention: the Lutheran, the Calvinist, and the Unitarian. Francis David, the founder of the Unitarian branch, had been both a Lutheran and a Calvinist before developing the doctrines of Unitarianism. And he had been originally trained for the Catholic priesthood! Francis David was a great sixteenth-century man, a seeker *and* a finder! In the century of exploration and discovery, Francis David was a worthy companion to Johannes Kepler, Christopher Columbus, and William Shakespeare.

Two more meetings were held, before Francis David convinced the prince that Unitarianism should be the official religion of Transylvania. The way I first heard the story, in its concise, popularized form, was that the prince convened the heads of all the churches and asked them what they would do if they were made official. The Catholic replied that he would insure the complete triumph of Catholicism by persecuting all others. The Lutheran and the Calvinist had basically the same idea. Only the Unitarian said that he would tolerate all the faiths and let everyone practice in peace.

This mythical version is relatively accurate, but for one glaring omission: the religion of the Romanian peasants, Greek Orthodoxy was not recognized among the faiths that were going to be protected. In the end, this omission led to the end of Hungarian princely rule in Transylvania. I mention this because it is a fact of extreme importance even today.

Francis David's Unitarian movement was originally known as the Anti-Trinitarian church because its thesis was that God was one, not "four or five Gods." And I quote from a summary of David's views:

> There is only one Father for whom and by whom is everything . . . outside of this God there is no other God, neither three, neither four, neither in substance, neither in persons, because the Scripture nowhere teaches anything about a triple God.

Later on, Francis David says that Jesus was a man, the son of God, certainly, but not God.

I certainly like that idea. In my opinion Jesus was not just the son of God, but an abused Son of God. There are grounds for a child-abuse trial here. But this is not my church, sorry.

Anyway, at the third debate, the views of the Unitarian prevailed, and Transylvania became the freest, most tolerant region of Europe for a brief, but significant time. In 1571 Unitarianism reached the peak of its popularity with almost five hundred congregations. After Prince Sigismund died, intolerance, which was more the norm, seized the day again. The Calvinists condemned Unitarianism and imprisoned Francis David. He died in prison in 1579. The brief exercise in part-time religious tolerance ended, but Unitarianism made a permanent mark in Transylvania and became ingrained in its consciousness.

Now, for those of you who have never been to Transylvania, and know it only from the very bad movies about Dracula, here are a few facts: Transylvania is a mountainous region in the center of Romania. It is a multiethnic area with a majority of Romanians, most of whom are still Christian Orthodox, a Hungarian minority, which is both Catholic and Protestant, and a shrinking German minority, which is for the most part Catholic. My birth town, Sibiu, not far from Alba Iulia, was founded by Saxon Germans shortly after the year 1000. There are still a few Jews left in Transylvania but they, for the most part, perished in World War II, or emigrated to Israel after the war.

The chief feature of the Transylvania region is its beauty. One can find here the height of Romanian village culture. Villages such as Răşinari and Sălişte near Sibiu are models of an ecological universe that exists in few places in the world anymore, a universe which has survived—though barely—the industrial ravages of four decades of careless state planning. The mountain peaks and valleys where these villages are nestled are some of the most beautiful alpine landscapes on earth. It is a wonder, and perhaps a saving grace, that the skiers and tourists of the world have not yet discovered these bejeweled scapes. The Transylvanian cities, particularly Sibiu, Brasov, Cluj, Sighişoara, and Alba Iulia, are historical treasures, in great need of attention. Restoration efforts have been sporadic for lack of money.

Transylvania, just as Bram Stoker's imagination told him, based on the descriptions of travelers, is a place of magic, legends, and fairy tales. The rich Romanian, Hungarian, and German folklore that is found here gives you a clue to the richness and complexity of its people's inner lives.

To give you only one example, it is said that my home town of Sibiu is the place where the Pied Piper of Hamelin took the children he piped away from Saxony. It is a most believable tale to anyone who has sat at sunset looking over the Cibin River, past the slanted rooftops with the blinking eyes, at the tall Carpathian peaks in the distance. I spent my childhood dreaming by mossy old walls, looking up at towers, climbing up steps from one side of the town to the other. Anyone looking down on the city from the Liars' Bridge will be seized by a keen sense of history. Many things happened here. They left behind the husk of their wisdom, traces, scents. (Incidentally, the Liars' Bridge is so named because this is where lovers stood, for centuries, whispering sweet lies to each other.)

And, speaking of lies, let us not get too carried away by sentiment. Transylvania, this physical multicultural paradise, is not much of a paradise these days.

When I grew up, I had Hungarian and German friends. It never occurred to us that we should hate each other. We went to school together, we hung together and, occasionally, we even made fun of each others' quirky expressions and funny clothes. But we spoke each other's languages and were taught to respect each other's dances, music, and poetry. We lived in a world made rich by each other's traditions, made richer, in fact, because we didn't have a whole lot of things. We were materially poor, but our souls were quite well fed.

After the collapse of Ceauşescu's authoritarian regime in 1989, there were ugly developments. Ethnic hatred made its overt appearance for the first time in decades. Romanians and Hungarians, who had gotten along like cranky relatives during the authoritarian period, began to deride each other openly. The Germans began to emigrate massively to Germany, leaving entire deserted communities behind. The Gypsies became the object of persecution for everyone. And in a place with a very poor history of tolerance for Jews, and very few Jews left, anti-Semitism reared its ugly head again.

There were incidents of violence where people were killed. In the town of Tîrgu-Mureş, where Hungarians are in the majority, an ethnic riot broke out. The mayor of Cluj, Koloszvar in Hungarian, the largest city in Transylvania, is a Romanian nationalist named Funar. He has incurred the wrath of the Hungarians with his numerous anti-Hungarian provocations.

I will refrain from assigning blame to any group, but it is clear that interethnic hatred is being encouraged both in Romania and Hungary by irresponsible nationalists who coincide—surprise! surprise!—with members of the old secret police in both countries. Hungarians in Transylvania have legitimate demands, which have been ignored in the past by Ceaușescu's nationalist policies. After 1989, the old party and police apparatchiks, afraid of losing power, began invoking the old demons of hatred, a sure way to appeal to people's emotions, and to bypass their hungry stomachs.

As the disastrous economy of Romania got worse, the strident need to blame someone grew. The Romanian nationalists blamed the Hungarians for their problems. Everyone, Romanians and Hungarians, began blaming Gypsies and Jews, the perennial targets of European stupidity. This situation, incidentally, was replicated, with varying degrees of intensity, all over the prolapsed ex-Commie fiefdom. The most intense form of it can be witnessed in Bosnia-Herzegovina, where fascist-Communist Serbs tried to destroy every living Muslim, and in a milder form in Poland where President Walesa tried to lure foreign investors by promising them a "homogenous country," i.e., a country without Jews.

You need have only a minimal recall of history to understand that there is nothing funny about the new European nationalist fascism, whether in Transylvania or in Bosnia-Herzegovina. The same explosive mix of ethnicity exists in patchwork form all over former Red Europe. Red was bad enough, but when they turn green and black, look out!

Transylvania today is not the place where the Unitarian values of tolerance and inclusion are particularly active. The Unitarian Church in Transylvania is ethnically Hungarian. Unlike the Unitarian Churches in the United States, there are no other nationalities in the church. No Romanians, Germans, Gypsies, or Jews among them. Their attitude toward women leaves quite a bit to be desired.

I understand the need of the American church to root itself in a historic tradition, to take hold of its history. But before claiming such roots, before even building buildings for its ancient kin, it must ask some hard questions.

Given the principle of tolerance affirmed in Transylvania and practiced in America, how tolerant is the Transylvanian church toward other ethnic groups?

Would they welcome, let's say, Romanians?

How about Jews?

What was the position of the Unitarian Church during World War II when Transylvania was under Hungarian control and when its entire Jewish population was deported to Auschwitz?

Did the Unitarian Church do anything to help those doomed by the authorities?

What is the Unitarian Church doing today in the spirit of tolerance, acceptance, and love?

These are hard questions, but American Unitarians must ask them. If there is any real connection between the Transylvanian Unitarian church and its American present-day form beyond a romantic wish for an ancient history, this connection has to be reinforced by the values of our day.

It's nice to have a history but it's better to have principles. It is up to the American church to hold to its principles of tolerance, openness, inclusion, and community, as models to the ancient kin.

When I spoke to a Unitarian in Boston recently, she explained her congregation's work in Transylvania this way: "If we were Catholic, we would help in Rome. We are Unitarians, so we go help in Transylvania."

That's a nice way to put it, but Transylvania is not Rome, no matter how much people might wish it. Rome is all Catholic and the Pope lives there. Transylvania is part of a country called Romania. Many people live there. They should all be helped, even if it is only by helping some who believe that you should help all. If there is even a shred of doubt in anybody's mind that helping the Unitarians of Transylvania creates discord and dissatisfaction among others, the church must do other good works to compensate. If there is the slightest doubt that Unitarian work contributes to separatism and suspicion of others, the church must correct the situation in the American spirit of love and tolerance. It is good that American Unitarians are contributing to the economy of Transylvania by building churches and helping people in need. But, please, do not succumb to the illness of naïveté, of which people around the world always accuse Americans. If there are problems, address them. Help foster understanding not separatism.

Unfortunately, Transylvania is full, these days, of people who like to see flaws instead of beauty. They live in beauty, but they do not know it.

Eastern **Europe**

Forgotten

At the height of interest in Eastern Europe, some of us thought that interest in Eastern Europe was high. That was a mistake. The American people were not that interested. The media was. I wrote a book about the dramatic events in Romania in 1989, which culminated with the execution of the dictator, Nicolae Ceauşescu. Shortly after that, I gave a talk to an interested group and someone asked me a question. He began, "Can you tell us, Mr. Ceauşescu . . . ?" People laughed, I laughed. "Codrescu," I said. "Like secret *code* and *rescue* at sea. . . ." Oh.

Nowadays, whenever someone mistakes my name for that of the dead dictator, I take it as a good sign. At least, they remember *something*. Media-induced amnesia is increasing geometrically on any issue, but in the case of Eastern Europe, with its myriad of difficulties and consonants, amnesia is instant. What we are supposed to remember and what we are supposed to forget used to be dictated by the delicate gravity of a moral response. One usually remembered what was important in one's scheme of things. But nowadays that scheme of things no longer contains a clear picture of priorities.

So it's no surprise when General Powell says that the U.S. shouldn't have gotten involved in the Balkans to begin with. He is not only reflecting the people's desire to forget the area, he is anticipating their plea to be spared the mess altogether. If there is nothing to remember, there will be nothing to forget. Unfortunately, there is plenty hanging over us whether we remember or not: mass graves of civilians, mass rapes, shelling of city markets in Bosnia, razing of Chechen towns by Russian troops. Underscoring these dramas are economies in shambles, unemployment, fascist gangs, new mafias, unsteady nuclear weapons. And underlining all of it is a swelling ocean of bad feelings, a mixture of wounded national prides, disappointment in the West, nostalgia for dictatorships, fear, and fragmentation. These things are yet nameless and we couldn't remember them if we wanted to. But one day they will have names. And ranks. And serial numbers.

The **Meat** in **Motion**

Part 4

Saving **Steps**

T his guy was partaking of eggs Sardou on the porch at the Columns and as I went past him, he went *pssst.* I unwillingly sidled over and he beckoned me to sit. He was a trim type with a mission: "Listen," he rasped, "can't we skip a few steps and have a nice world?"

"Sure," I said, "but everyone can't live on eggs Sardou and ponder such questions. Some of us have to work, you know."

"Okay," he said, "but look at it this way. This guy in Florida kills a gynecologist so he won't kill babies and now we want to kill him for killing the gynecologist for killing. Couldn't we skip a couple of steps here so that nobody'd get killed?"

"Sure," I said, "but that's called reason, and we've run out of that stuff in this country eons ago. Besides, Florida didn't kill him, just put him away for two lifetimes, whatever that means."

But the stranger was relentless. "And think of this law that just passed in the West somewhere that requires prisoners to work at jobs to pay for their upkeep. They'll be competing with free people for scarce jobs so that those people will now have to commit crimes that will land them in jail where they'll have to work to pay for their upkeep. Couldn't we skip a couple of steps here and just give people jobs in the first place?" I agreed that we could, and I was about to skip a few steps out of there myself, when he grabbed my arm: "And how about that minister who was so afraid of the Brady Law he bought a whole lot of guns and then shot himself dead at dinner while showing his family how to use guns safely? Couldn't he have skipped a couple of steps here?"

"In this case," I said, "he couldn't have. If he hadn't shot himself at dinner in front of his family we wouldn't have known that God was against guns."

"I don't understand," my interlocutor said, "didn't you skip a couple of steps here?"

"I'm sure I did," I said, "but I'm late for a training seminar in living with the absurd and, 'sides, your eggs Sardou are getting cold."

"And how about the guy who shot at the White House and got arrested, and then Jesse Helms threatened the President and barely apologized? Couldn't we have skipped. . . ." Maybe, but I never heard the rest.

The Mafia Was Appalled

At what point exactly does politics-as-entertainment become politics-as-horror-show? The answer to this question, Louisiana-style, has been coming fast and furious. The FBI just shined the light on dozens of legislators on the payroll of the video-poker industry. The slimy web involves lawmakers, their wives, their children, county officials, sheriffs, lobbyists, and businessmen. The scale of this outrage surpasses even the unassailable standards of sleaze established by past Louisiana politicians. The trouble is that gambling modifies the scale: it makes everything worse, even sleaze. We are now at a point where, as a cabdriver told me, "even the Mafia is appalled by the greed of Louisiana politicians."

Gambling is America's most pernicious current disease. Touted as a panacea for urban ills, it is in fact quite the opposite. It sucks disposable income from the community, it fosters despair, it increases crime, it makes the corruptible downright rotten. And unlike Louisiana itself, it has zero entertainment value. It preys on the ignorant and the addicted. Families have been decimated by this addiction and addict self-help groups are mushrooming. Oddly enough, the only good guy in this latest *affaire* is the state police commission, which has been trying to check the peddlers of video crack. Its work, though, isn't quite sufficient to take the shudder out of the word *police*.

The New Orleans Police Department has been providing the nation with its own horror show. There may even be a suspected serial killer in its ranks. The romance of Louisiana as a refuge for riverboat gamblers, pirates, and cutthroats is no romance these days. The mix of rotten politicians, murderer cops, and ruthless gangsters is a gold mine only for writers. For everybody else it's a cesspool.

Airplanes and What to Make of 'Em

I've been taking enough airplanes this month to acquire a light coating of aluminum and a skewed sense of time. My inner clock, after being reset enough times, has just quit working. It's stuck on midnight, which is when, if I'm lucky, I can lie down. Therefore, I always feel like lying down, and think that I am, even when in fact I'm up and talking. Every airline has its own style of friendly banter that helps nothing. In the friendly skies of Delta they thank you so many times for being there you want to throw something at them. On Northwest they give you a bag of peanuts or, if you're lucky, a gooey lump of dough, and they try to point out interesting things along the way whether it's cloudy or not. Continental has a brisker style that would be almost refreshing if it wasn't so inane. My favorite line from the captain of an airship so far was on takeoff when he called out: "Miss Earhart, I have your purse in the cockpit!"

And God forbid if you've left your book behind. The airline magazines, with the exception of crossword puzzles and ads for new types of suitcases, are fuller of mind bubble gum than the floors of a twenty-four-hour movie house. Profiles of public figures written with a view to reassuring everyone that stupidity is far from rare . . . travel articles to lovely places like China which fail to mention the type of government there . . . business advice for the brain-addled salesman who left his calculator back at the hotel . . . fashion spreads that you wouldn't want to be caught dead in when the plane crashes . . . on and on, words sucked dry of any juice they might have possessed.

And once you're out of these stingy tin cans full of canned air for the free circulation of bacilli, you find yourself at timelessly identical airports with their lousy newsstands and pizza counters and two hot dogs for a dollar. Surely, in this vastly energetic country, we could have nicer planes, better magazines, more interesting airports. Or is the industry aiming to achieve the standards of the Greyhound firm, which models itself, I believe, on the River Styx Canoe Company?

Girth and
Weirdness

Airplane seats are getting smaller while American behinds are growing larger. Levi's jeans, which knows these things, has been making bigger pants. Then why do airlines who also know these things make smaller seats? Is it just because they want to cram more people in the unsanitary tin cans that pass for airplanes these days? Or are they conducting an endurance experiment to see which airline can piss off more people? There was a time when taking an airplane seemed a reasonably comfortable way to travel, but it's no different from Greyhound now. I know, because I use both. Being crammed in coach between two cranky, fat people who'll get fed only peanuts until they get back to their neighborhood Shoney's two thousand miles away is not an unusual experience now, it's the norm. Some other new norms are: the bigger people get the less you feed them. And the crankier they get, the less attention you pay them. Greyhound too, packs them in like sardines, but at least you can get off the bus if you can't take it anymore.

And suppose you pay through your nose to sit in first class, do you think you've got it better? Not a chance. The seat's a bit bigger, it's true, just like coach seats ought to be, but it's just as packed and the people are even fatter. The only good thing is that they give you a tablecloth with your peanuts and wine so cheap it stains your teeth forever. I keep hearing talk about all these newfangled planes with TVs and computers in the seat arms, but the way things are going, I can't see where they are going to put these things unless they screw them directly into your head when you board the plane. You can add to this mix the fact that all domestic flights are nonsmoking now and you can be sure that at least one-third of the squeezed, underfed, and untended are also having a nicotine fit. Can barehanded strangling of airline crew be far behind? Is involuntary terrorism around the corner?

The **Life-Style** of
the **Puppet**

I t is possible to live in New York and never touch the ground. You can descend straight from the clouds into your waiting stretch limo, be ferried softly to and fro, and fed manna by discreet angels before you're even hungry. So, after I've become accustomed to this, I have to walk a half block and suffer indignities? Oh, sorry, wrong story. I *usually* walk and suffer indignities, but this time I got the clouds and the limo, and let me tell you, it's hell. I took the limo down to the depths of the Lower East Side where I used to live. I rolled out the door, expecting the street cats to raise their ski masks for a second with respect. Instead, one of them goes, "Who's *that?*," like he knows every movie star and every major wholesaler and I'm not one of them.

Okay, then, so see you later, suckers, and I'm off to Bouley in Tribeca, a restaurant rated as number one in New York, which is to say the world, if you're a restaurant. Though it's almost summer, the hallway at the Bouley is stocked with baskets of nearly rotten apples, which give off a pungent scent of autumn. Flowers are shedding on my appetizer, which costs the monthly salary of twenty Romanian engineers. The three clam shells sit in a swirl of brown sauce crossed with sprigs of rosemary. Inside each shell is a small oyster steamed with herbs lying atop a slightly heavier urchin, treated likewise with some other herbs. The oyster is denser than the urchin and it presses it down a little like a working-class man atop a conservatory school student. It tastes sudden, like a spurt of seltzer on a hot Mexican afternoon. And speaking of class, my fellow Bouleynese are men in jillion-dollar suits and women in black with pearls and they don't move or talk at all as they eat, they just pose there as if the waiters are working for the society page. I don't have time to explicate the egregiously exquisite entrée or the torte elevator, but when the limo took me back to the penthouse, I sunk into my black marble tub with a sigh. Can you hear it?

Hits on the Run

T he faster you travel the more com-
pressed the info you get. If you're in the California Bay Area for a few
minutes, for instance, you may hear that "Chez Panisse now charges for
reservations." Chez Panisse is a famous restaurant and, later, when you
deconstruct this, you understand that the fact that Chez Panisse charges
for reservations signals a whole new thing, some of which is a new thing
about restaurants—I mean, who ever heard of a restaurant charging for
reservations?—and also a new thing about fame in the nineties, namely
that if you're famous, whether you're a restaurant or a baseball player,
you can charge for things that were previously free, like reservations
and signatures.

If you go to Seattle, you are likely to hear that "We don't jaywalk in

Seattle," which can mean many things. It can mean that people here are law-abiding, as well as being still so laid back that they don't need to rush across the street like maniac New Yorkers whenever there is an opening in the traffic. It could also mean that Seattle drivers, pumped by caffeine and not completely weaned from their Western heritage of hunting and trapping, will run down a pedestrian like a lost mink.

Later, you go to Portland and, while you're still in the airport, you notice the newspaper headline, "Solar Cooking Hits the Northwest." You don't really have time to read the article for details but you can only imagine that, since the sun appears so rarely in the area, the natives have figured out yet another way to get the most out of it. They leave their eggs on the porch when they go to work. When they come home, presto, ten minutes of midday sun and the suckers are hard.

But certain things are constant, no matter where you travel in the U.S.A. today: espresso is everywhere and so is cyberspace, and they both happened at about the same time. Americans are being woken up with coffee for cybertravel and made to pay more for it, whether it's reservations or fame. Nothing is free anymore except the sun and it doesn't come out so much. And we obey the traffic lights. And when we travel as fast as I did through real space, we'd better ready our aphorism catcher. All you get is one insight per city.

Good **Vibrations**

I t's a clean, well-lighted place as Hemingway would have liked. The displays are well spaced and spare so that you can browse leisurely. A middle-aged woman and her daughter are taking turns weighing a hefty object called "the Jeff Striker" in their hands. "It has the texture and feel of the real thing," mother explains. "Of *some* real things," the daughter says doubtfully. A kindly grandmother with kinky white hair is studying the "hitachi double-head," which advertises its "versatility" as "perfect for sharing." Meeting the eye of a sympathetic stranger, grandma shakes her head at the difficulty of finding just the perfect gift for that special someone. In the end, she settles for a Tiffany "smoothie" in metallic silver. It's a reliable product, the original and popular 7½-inch long, 1¼-inch thick battery vibrator, available also in blue, pearl, pink, purple, white, and yellow.

Yes, it's lunchtime at Good Vibrations on Valencia Street in San Francisco and the girls are shopping for instruments of pleasure. The tastefully arranged window of this establishment is arrayed with some scary mechanical devices that had procured women pleasure in the dark ages of the past. Some of these rusted *objets* look like dentists' drills or lunatic restraints. The invention of electricity gave birth to some coily-looking things topped off by blunt spheres. Studying these products of illicit ingenuity one cannot help but feel grateful for the pastel-colored, silicone stimulators of our time. How can one not prefer the Willie Plug, for instance, or the Jane Wah, or the ever-popular G-spotter plus? And yet, there is something about the cheeriness of this market that is downright eerie, as if it was for aliens rather than humans. Maybe it's the shoppers' determined bravado that shouts, "It's my instrument and I'll play it any way I like." Or maybe it's the lack of anything dark, dirty, and forbidden. Whatever it is, the place feels oddly asexual, like a hardware store. The laundromat next door, full of half-dressed, sleepy people, is a lot sexier for some reason.

Twentysomething

A former student of mine I'll call Adrienne is a young lesbian who moved to San Francisco from Baton Rouge because she is twentysomething and San Francisco is where the scene is. Adrienne is now a certified teacher, but the best she could do in San Francisco was steaming milk in a cappuccino joint. And the scene didn't turn out quite the way she imagined, except once, which I'll tell you about shortly. She found a room for under five hundred dollars in the Sunset in a house full of other twentysomethings, two of whom are gay and two of whom are straight. Not that it much matters. Here is how Adrienne puts it:

"I'm really sick of it. Everyone's just like me. All we do is sit around and complain about how we can't find anybody and about how we have

all these college degrees and all we get is coffeehouse jobs. And everybody goes, 'What are you going to do when you grow up?' And I'm
twenty-six already! I have to move to a lesbian house in the Mission. I
need some other perspectives!"

What she means by "other perspectives" is simply older people who
may have a different attitude from her generation, which is, it seems,
gripped by an ennui that drives them to make holes in their bodies, tat-
too and brand their skin, paint their hair, in short, anything that *feels*
like something. Adrienne had a girlfriend for a while but then the girlfriend got a boyfriend the day she graduated from college. "She was just
a LUG," Adrienne says, "Lesbian Until Graduation."

For her own self, lesbianism seems so far to be about the only thing
that makes the tedium of fin de siècle bearable. But, who knows? The
only time since arriving in San Francisco that Adrienne really had a
great time the way she was supposed to be having was when this punk
girl handed her an invitation to a rave on Haight Street. She went, took
Extasy, and ended up experiencing the bliss and wonder of just touching the skin of strangers, amazed by the texture and color of an orange,
and just feeling young and luscious. "It's too bad," she said, "that one
of the girls had a seizure just after the orgy. It had to be the combination. She was doing heroin just before." It had to be the combination, I
agreed. And I added: "The combination of late capitalism, unfocused
nostalgia, and bad poetry."

"Sure," said Adrienne, "why not?"

Escorts

A writer's tour is like the Tour de France. You've got to be in shape. You won't get there typing. The only good thing about the tour is the tour story you get to write when you recover. I won't add to all the tour stories with my own tales of scary hotels, lunch-on-the-phone, fans who shaved their head for you, toothless autograph seekers, and so on. I'll praise my escorts instead. If you're lucky, you get Bill Young in Chicago. Bill drives a huge, old American car that he parks anywhere he feels like. When a traffic cop writes him a ticket, he rushes up to her and tells her that he's got a famous writer in the car, and then gives her a copy of your book. The cop is charmed, she tears up the ticket. Bill's charm is famous. One well-known writer prefers to sleep on his couch rather than in a fancy hotel because he values Bill's company over room service. Bill is a raconteur. He can tell a story.

He's not the only one. Lisa Maxon, in Denver, has some great ones. Escorts don't name names, but some of the writers she drove around were pretty peculiar. Of course, she's no average Joe herself: she eats the livers of antelopes and the hearts of elk her husband shoots in Wyoming. And she'll lend her wedding dress to a writer getting married. Her brand-new Cadillac talks back when you open the door. In Los Angeles, Karen Hebert likes to talk back at her car radio tuned in to all-talk AM. In Atlanta, Esther Levine can zip between appointments and take you to the rug sale of the century to get a present for your son. In Portland, Barbara Erlich offers cookies to everyone and is eagerly anticipated by two cookie-chomping seeing-eye dogs at the local public radio station. In Seattle, Deirdre Devlin gives you the rundown on every restaurant, including menu secrets known only to their chefs. She's the president of the local culinary association. And in San Francisco, there is Naomi Appel, a book writer herself, who doesn't have to escort anyone unless she likes his or her work. Her book is about writers' dreams, which they tell her as if she were their analyst. These people perform as instant moms and confidants: they soothe the weary writer and bind his wounds. They are a kind of martyr, too. You've never seen cranky if you've never seen a writer in midtour.

Thank you, folks.

Find Your **Bed** Crowded

When I decided to enter the gothic arena, it was only natural. It was almost a birthright. After all, Transylvania, where I was born, gave the world Dracula and Ceauşescu. And that's only two dark figures in a region that teems with them. When a Transylvanian child grows up he or she gets to view the pantheon of this inheritance and choose a ghastly figure to take into the world. It provides the child with an advantage, a head start. I chose Countess Elisabeth Bathory of Hungary who is alleged to have bathed in the blood of 650 virgin girls in order to keep her beauty and insure her immortality. By Transylvanian standards she is not all that gruesome. Somewhere, let's say, between Zsa Zsa Gabor, Tammy Faye Bakker, and Jeffrey Dahmer. So I brought Countess Bathory to life and started my book tour.

Imagine my surprise when I found that the slight head start that a Transylvanian monster gives you has all but vanished. Right ahead of me, leading a team of vampires, was Anne Rice. At a book signing she jumped out of a coffin in a bridal gown. Thousands of book-buying vampires were waiting for her. I realized then that just having a monster is not enough: you must give people a reason to dress up.

In such a situation, there are only a few options. My friend Barry Gifford suggested that I mud wrestle with Anne Rice on the Letterman show. "Go for the thighs!" he advised. Another option is to hire Bathorettes, young virgins with a drop of blood on their necks, to do the Cajun step behind me at book signings. And another yet is to slip the book to Bob Dole who can trash it on TV. That would be good because the book is a ten on the Bob Dole scale of sex and violence. Mostly sex, though, surprisingly enough. Another thought is to tie Countess Bathory in to O.J., Susan Smith, and Jeffrey Dahmer—but I won't. Even pushed to the limit, Transylvanians have their pride.

Bird **Brains** and Al **Capone**

Someone said to me, while I watched a big gambling boat suck and spew suckers in St. Louis, "Did you know that birds shed their brains when they migrate?" I didn't know that but seeing the tourists being swallowed by the casino, I could believe it.

My interlocutor was birdlike himself, a Chicago salesman who had been spending so much time on the road, he had begun studying migratory birds in an effort to understand himself. There is an unspoken solidarity among us travelers. We recognize each other instantly by our fatigue-rimmed eyes, an air of resignation capable of turning at once into sardonic amusement, and a certain way of feeling at home in places that are clearly not: hotel lobbies, airports, tourist traps, balconies over gussied-up rivers. We can begin to converse at any point in any given train of thought, even begin in midsentence, and it would be all right.

"In fact," I said, "the animatronic figure of Al Capone would be right at home here!"

The bird man nodded. I had just come from Chicago where I'd spent an hour in a strange mechanical theater dedicated to Al Capone. It had been built by some amusement company that ignored Al Capone's actual digs, which were decaying unnoticed down the street.

Travelers will often meet in the neutral nowheres that are their temporary homes and will bring each other news of their respective cities. The bird man had just come from New Orleans where, he told me, they were almost done building the new casino. And I had just come from Chicago where I'd seen the Capone show he hadn't yet seen. It was a service, really: I would never go into the New Orleans casino and he'd probably never set foot in the Al Capone theater. We did these dirty jobs for each other. Like migratory birds we shed our brains and passed on the news. "Did you know that there is winter on the sun?" "That fish have antifreeze to keep them moving?"

We would have kept on like this, but were drowned by two separate flocks of tourists. One of them massed about a bellhop and asked him if they could get on the gambling boat at that hour. "No," he said, "they must stimulate like they're sailing," which meant, I believe, that the stationary boat had to pretend that it was sailing to meet local laws.

The other was a flock of doctors' wives greeting a shuttle that would take them to a plane that would take them to a New Age fat farm in Tucson, Arizona. It was a shared moment and we, long-distance birds, soared briefly above the garden-variety warblers.

We parted without good-byes.

Another **Big** Question

With vacation looming, the big question is: How does a workaholic acquire the grace of slack? How does one hold at bay that sinking feeling when it's nearly one P.M. and the phone hasn't rung once? I want to imagine myself disconnected from the phone, free of the fax, unplugged from the computer, far from the intercom, days away from overnight delivery, pardoned from the doorbell, unworried about reservations, careless about reception and delivery, wireless, bar-codeless, modemless.

See, that's me, over there on that patch of hot sand on the desert island with nary a lonely cloud above it, let alone a helicopter, blimp, or balloon. Nothing here but me and this tuft of grass under attack by a solitary ant with a dream. A dream of carrying the whole tuft to some underground office and hoping to get it there before noon. No, better not study ants. They are workaholics. Better to watch that gull in free, easy flight over the ripply, blue mirror of ocean, diving for a fish. Oh, yes, it's feeding time in gull-sky, it's always feeding time in gull-sky, the stomach is like a gaping voice-mail box, full of fish, and still ready to take on more. Forget the gulls, watch the turtles. There goes one, or rather, there sits one, immobile like the essence of slack itself, dreaming dreams of the Void. I am turtle, I repeat after myself. And at that very moment, the turtle gets up on those fat turtle legs and takes off at six hundred miles an hour along an invisible telegraph wire. Of course, even a real turtle would run from a workaholic.

The beach is not the answer. Maybe the woods. But I hear they've put cellular phones under mushrooms. And that mossy patch you're lying on is really the lid over a factory full of underground atomic workers.

I need a slack teacher.

The **Tedium** of Self

T he editor of a travel magazine
asked me to write some stories about places I go to. Sure, I said, but I
can't do 'em in the first person. There is a character inside me who's a
much better traveler than me. His name is Pen, and he is a better observer, a sharper wit, and a classier dude all around. For instance, last
year at Marienbad, the Pen found himself face to face with a maître d'
who disapproved of his blue jeans. The Pen drew himself up to the up-
permost point of his nib and demanded to see the owner of the establishment. The owner, a sour dwarf in an Armani three-piece with several
jangling gold chunks on his fingers and around his neck, was illiterate
but guilty about it. When the Pen explained that he was the author of
several highly regarded volumes of difficult verse, he was given dis-

pensation and seated by the window with a view to the pale green Mediterranean. It was an overcast day and the *bouillabaisse* was over-rated. Still, it was better than what one might find anywhere else. The mussels held the fresh flavor of the Mediterranean sun within the ten-der firmness of their pulp, and the other *coquilles* were matched per-fectly to the garlic and the extra-virgin olive oil. The Pen considered this dish to be the epitome of the Franco-Italian spirit, that civilized hy-brid of sun, olives, and poetry.

The Pen doesn't have a mission. In fact, he doesn't even have any business. His purpose is to be amused. "The word *amuse* contains the muse," he often tells those of his acquaintances sporadically seized by curiosity. "And the muse is the force that drives this Pen," he concludes grandly. The Pen travels because he is curious. He is arch though quite tolerant, he finds human foibles endearing, but is unforgiving of pre-tention. What a crank!

The Pen, of course, is not alone, I told the editor. He keeps company with all sorts of portly, unmusical and lazy characters in me. Together they keep the tedium of self at bay. *I,* as Rimbaud said, *is another.* And another. And one more.

The **Coca**-Cola Museum

I went to the Coca-Cola Museum in Atlanta and saw the past and the future amid a mass of squealing, squeaky kids. First of all, just as they tell you in the lobby, Coca-Cola is not just a drink. It's America. It started out as a cocaine-laced energy booster that depicted, in its first ads, deliriously energetic housewives leaping over themselves to get to the soda fountain for a fix. Later, they took the cocaine out, but left in enough caffeine and sugar to cause future generations of youth to leap over great obstacles at a single bound. Since 1886, Coca-Cola ads have depicted an American history that is both real and idealized. The real parts are quite vivid: they include the remains of the Victorian age, the great depression, World War II, the early space age, rock 'n' roll, urban guerrilla chic. Surrounding this history like fanciful dantelle is a caffeine-fueled optimism, reflected in the art-nouveauish bodies of the twenties, fascist deco of the thirties, stylish, body-fitting uniforms during the war, space-booster futurism, and so on. The America that Coca-Cola has given us is overly, perhaps insanely, optimistic and, above all, energetic. Americans, Coca-Cola tells us, are sexier, faster, stronger, tougher, and just plain better.

These are the very same values that Communist ideologues tried to indoctrinate in their youths but failed. Which goes to show you: words without cocaine or caffeine are like eggs without salt, bumping without grinding, drinking without swallowing.

The Coca-Cola Museum jumps from Norman Rockwell nostalgia to space-age futurism without missing a beat. In the process it takes in the world. A display of soda fountains from around the world spritzes exotic colas, like Lichee Nut Cola, into outstretched paper cups. The kids go bananas here, knocking back foreign-language colas as if they were dew drops. The floor is sticky and the kids are full of caffeine. Things look good.

Father and Son Undertake Search for Brujo

When my son, Tristan, was thirteen and a half he started reading the Don Juan books by Carlos Castaneda and became a very serious young man. "The trouble with you," he said, "is that you have too much self-importance!"

I defended myself as best I could. Surely, he couldn't have meant that I was a selfish, self-absorbed individual just because I spend between thirteen and fourteen hours a day typing in my attic, to emerge only when I need a crust of bread and a drink. That's not selfish, that's insane. There is a difference. I noticed also that he accused me of self-importance only when I disagreed with him. "Sure," I said, "being thirteen and a half means that everything your father does is wrong. How about *your* self-importance, you conceited little brat?"

Very adult conversation. By the time he got to the end of the fourth volume of Carlos Castaneda's adventures in the spirit worlds of Mexican shamans, Tristan had a new mission. He needed to find a "teacher" somewhere in the desert to teach him how to fly and other nifty things that Don Juan taught to his pupil Carlos. I tried telling him that math was more important at the moment than flying but that was just further proof of my terminal self-importance. If the truth be known, I don't really think that math is more important than flying. On the contrary. But I didn't really want to tell him that or he'd give up on math altogether. When I was his age I thought *anything* was more important than math. Watching a fly crawl up the chalk on my teacher's desk, for instance.

One day there was an item in the newspaper that made Tristan very excited. He'd been a faithful reader of the comics and sports pages ever since he discovered that if he propped the paper against his cereal bowl he wouldn't have to talk to his parents in the morning. On this day, however, he read the front part for some reason. I wasn't too thrilled about that. That's *my* part of the paper. Call it self-importance if you will, but I need to be the first to know about earthquakes and other important things. Anyway, I let it pass, and Tristan discovered the Item.

The Item said that on Columbus Day, Native American shamans from North and South America were going to the pyramids at Teotihuacán near Mexico City to hold ceremonies of mourning to mark five hundred years since Columbus came over here and ruined their lives forever. Tristan said that he had to go. He would, if necessary, mow every lawn on the block and empty every pencil holder in the house to buy himself a plane ticket. I tried to talk him out of it. I pointed out to him that he had school, that he couldn't go by himself, that I had work to do, and that if Columbus hadn't come someone else would have and done the same thing. That was probably the worst thing to say. Tristan is so politically correct he makes me sound like Archie Bunker. He thinks animals and trees have priority over people. Polluters should be shot. The young are wiser than the old. Dress codes are stupid. It's funny. I used to have those ideas myself.

His fourteenth birthday was coming up, so in a moment of weakness I said, "Heck, what's a few days of school? Let's go to the pyramids for Columbus Day!"

That was that. We did. Tristan packed about two dozen tapes of alternative music, four Carlos Castaneda books, two pairs of jeans, and a couple of T-shirts. On the plane he wore his NUN MOLESTERS T-shirt, which earned him some dirty looks from a couple of sisters flying on a mission of mercy somewhere. Not that he noticed. He listened to Concrete Blonde on his earphones all the way from New Orleans to Mexico. I tried pointing out clouds and rivers in the hope of making the trip instructional as well as amusing, but the concrete blondes prevented him from overhearing my pedagogical asides.

In the cab to the city we read the Spanish on the billboards and had a lot of fun trying to figure them out. He had some Spanish but it was pretty basic. He could say, "¡Gracias a Díos, hay arroz!," which means, I think, "Thank God, we have rice." It's a good phrase but its usefulness is rather limited. I mean, under what circumstances do you actually say, "Thank God, we have rice?" "Well, maybe," Tristan said, "you're stuck in the jungle without a clue on how to get back to civilization but it's okay because ¡Gracias a Díos, hay arroz!" I agreed that this might be useful in that particular case but I pointed out that the jungles of Mexico, such as they were, were greatly outnumbered by cities, skyscrapers, resort hotels, and TV sets.

We put up at a hotel in the Zona Rosa in Mexico City and went for a walk on the Avenida de la Reforma. The wonderful smell of frying tortillas and diesel fuel that is peculiar to the city hit me at once and filled me with nostalgic memories. Every city has its own smell. Paris smells like coffee, cigarettes, and newspapers. New Orleans smells like fried shrimp and powdered sugar. Bucharest, Romania, smells like crumbling plaster, linden flowers and lilac eau de cologne. I would like to write a smell guide to the cities I've been to, about the memories these smells evoke.

Last time I'd been to Mexico City, Tristan had been only four years old and he had been deadly afraid of the Punk Police. I asked him if he remembered the Punk Police. He didn't. I remembered them very well. We were having dinner in a nice restaurant with our friends Philip and Mike. Tristan decided to crawl under the dignified feet of the well-dressed diners and to startle them. Polite attempts to keep him in his seat failed so Philip told him about the Punk Police. The Punk Police, he said, are charged with the duty of arresting children who crawl under diners' feet in the finer restaurants. There were immediate results. Unfortunately, every time the restaurant door opened Tristan saw a potential Punk Policeman and hid under my arm.

Now, here we were, ten years later, and he had an earring in his ear, long hair, and a real attitude about the police. He commented snidely on their ubiquity. He didn't like the T-shirts young Mexicans were wearing, either. "Nothing but lousy heavy metal!" he exclaimed. I said that

Mexicans had wonderful folk music of their own, and that the groups advertised on their T-shirts were only superficial imports from us. In fact, the shamans, when we were going to encounter them, probably made their own music on homemade flutes and pipes.

Early next morning we went to the ethnography museum in Chapultepec Park to look at pre-Columbian art. I explained that it would come in handy in identifying shamans. Their faces, symbols, and rituals were carved in the ancient stone. Meanwhile, the real faces, new symbols, and recent rituals of contemporary Mexicans were all around us. It was Sunday and families were out in force, strolling, listening to musicians, and eating ice cream. Chapultepec Park is one of the world's greatest family playgrounds. It is immense. We lounged on the edge of a fountain and watched four Indian pole dancers. They threw themselves off from the top of a high pole with only a rope around their waists and flew above our heads playing their flutes. Tristan was impressed.

"In the old days," I said, "this dance was performed only for ritual purposes to establish the unity of the world by bringing together the four cardinal points."

"Now," he said, "they do it for money."

Right. Still, it was a good show. Before we got to the Ethnography Museum we watched a whole family of clowns put on their makeup before doing a show. "Clowns are scary!" Tristan said. They didn't look scary to me, but then I hadn't read Stephen King's *It*. That book had apparently given him a bad case of clownophobia.

The stone gods of the Toltecs, Maya, and Aztecs loomed above us in the grand halls of the Anthropology Museum. I have always felt a mixture of dread and unease before these massive figures from the ancient world. No one understands these cultures very well. The Spanish priests burned all the Aztec and Mayan books, leaving us only this writing in stone. Some of it has been read and understood, but most of it remains mysterious. Artifacts from the pyramids ranged from earthly familiar to outer-space alien. A huge stone face belonging to the rain god Tlaloc attracted Tristan's attention. He sat down cross-legged before it. I let him meditate and strolled on past stone jaguars, mighty snakes, demonic fish women, decapitated warriors, feathered suns, and moons with cat faces. A mammoth square of stone depicted an Aztec ball game. The winning players were sacrificed to the gods after the game. It was a real honor, apparently. They say that this game, played on a court with a ball, was the precursor of baseball. Happily, we dropped the honor.

When I looked for Tristan I found him very disturbed. He had meditated before Tlaloc, then he had given Quetzalcoatl a thoughtful pause, after which he had tuned in to a number of much scarier gods and goddesses. We walked outside toward the replica of a Mayan pyramid. Tristan said, "The Aztecs were evil sorcerers, that's what killed them."

As I opened my mouth to start asking him what made him think so, there was a whirl of colorful feathers and a bird fell dead at our feet. I'm not big on signs but this one was the size of a pyramid. Without a word, we headed for the edge of the fountain in the courtyard. A velvet black and yellow butterfly appeared from somewhere and danced in front of Tristan. They communed for a while and his mood improved immediately. The dead bird sent by the Aztec sorcerers to impede his progress had been neutralized by the butterfly.

Next day, we took a tour bus to the pyramids at Teotihuacán. The bus was full of mostly American tourists with a sprinkling of French and German passengers. Tristan sat at the back reading Carlos Castaneda. It was a beautiful, crisp day. The light was the color of ripe, golden corn. The sky was turquoise blue. We drove past fields of corn, a plant engineered by the ancient Americans to feed themselves. It ended up feeding the world. Moving in and out of the corn were the remains of a wall that had contained an Aztec lake of desalinized water. The wall had separated fresh from salt water. A sixteenth-century Spanish church sat on top of a hill surveying lands that had been expropriated by the Mexican state in the eighteenth century. Slums of roofless or tin-roofed adobes clung to the sides of mountains above Mexico City, testifying to the great wave of humanity that had been migrating to the city decade after decade. Now and then I saw people walking slowly behind burros laden with firewood. Little girls walked hand in hand on dusty roads. They payed no attention to the shiny, new tour bus whizzing past. We could have been a UFO.

When we stopped for a few minutes, a tiny man drew us into a demonstration he was making of the magical maguey plant. He peeled back parts of it with a sharp knife. The maguey produces *pulque*, Mexico's national wine, paper to write on, threads for weaving, needles to weave with, drinking glasses, and other things. It is a truly miraculous plant, a horn of plenty. Tristan asked the man in English if the maguey also produces psychedelic drugs, and the man nodded yes. The French tourists took their picture next to a burro with a straw hat on. A yellow dog wandered up from under a clothesline laden with drying synthetic shirts next to an adobe hut. A soldier with an old rifle stood sleepily on the other side of the road looking as if he'd forgotten the reason why he had been posted there. From where we were stopped we could see the great pyramids of Teotihuacán sailing over the vast plains like mysterious ships.

It began to rain lightly when we reached them. They were impressive, the pyramids, a whole immense city of ceremonial buildings whose purpose remains mysterious. The ancient Aztecs did not build them, they found them just the way they are now. They were built by a people we know nothing about, people who had come and vanished without a trace. When we set foot in the sacred city, I heard flutes, pipes, wind, rain, and the sound of ancient Indian languages. A cloud of vendors clad in native costumes descended on us with replicas of pre-Columbian faces, clay flutes with Aztec gods recumbent, heavy crystal globes, black soapstone eggs, Aztec calendars carved in wood or volcanic stone, cloth paintings, hammered silver bells, raised copper minipyramids, bamboo panpipes of many sizes, spun-glass replicas of the Niña, Pinta, and Santa Maria. . . . I waved them away, overwhelmed, but Tristan bought a clay flute and brought a few mournful notes out of it.

We walked up the long Avenue of the Dead toward the Pyramids of the Sun and the Moon. We descended and ascended worn stone steps rising out of large, sunken fields that could have once been filled with water. The houses of priests, temples, and markets must have stood on the shores of these walled lakes. They must have traveled on rafts up and down the watery roads. Mexico City had been a city of canals like Venice at the time Cortez arrived with the Spanish conquistadores in the sixteenth century. Teotihuacán, the sacred city of pyramids, could have also been a city on water. We climbed laboriously up the Pyramid of the Sun. It was a serious effort. On all sides of us, defeated tourists leaned out of breath against old stones. From the top we could see the great valley between the mountains surrounding us on all sides. The steps we had ascended were invisible and we felt as if we were standing on a small platform at the top of the world ready to take flight. "Yes," Tristan said. "This is more like it." I had to agree. It beat math.

We spotted the Native American runners. They were standing about a mile down in the middle of a site known as the Field of Ceremonies. There didn't seem to be many of them. They were outnumbered by the tourists who had no idea that today, exactly five hundred years ago, a man named Christopher Columbus had taken the New World under the cruel banner of Old World Spain. The Europeans, of course, didn't hold the copyright on cruelty. As we headed for the ceremonial we passed the Aztec ball courts and the sacrificial mounds atop of which Aztec priests cut out the hearts of their victims and dedicated them to the gods. On these mounds and at the bottom of the dry lakes we crossed there were now great circular empires of sand built by red ants. We carefully avoided stepping into the circles into whose centers they were busily burrowing. Some ancient Native Americans, like the Hopi, worshipped ants. But here, in the Aztec world, snakes had reigned supreme. The patterns on the side of the pyramids, on the walls of the temples, and on the stairs were formed by millions of small stones arranged in snake patterns.

The drizzle intensified as we approached the circle of Native American runners from North and South America who were meeting here for a day of mourning. Representatives of tribes exchanged ritual staffs and chanted the names of their places of origin. After each name, the participants lifted their hands to the sky and chanted the name over and over. These were the names of regions once inhabited by the native people of America. Places like Jalisco and Los Angeles. It was hard to imagine. A medicine woman burned incense in the middle of the grounds. A few hippies gone native walked about with babies in papooses smoking peace pipes. We could have been in California at some gathering of the tribes, but we were not. We were at the center of the Aztec civilization, it was Columbus day, and it was raining.

Tristan wrapped himself in his black cloak and sat on the ground with his legs crossed, his eyes closed. I listened to the rain and the wind carrying the mournful sound of Indian flutes and I felt a great sadness and longing. My longing was not for the vanished worlds of the Native Americans, though these too moved me and touched my heart, but for the wonder of being fourteen years old and experiencing deeply the mysteriousness of the world, its bittersweet poetry.

By the time we returned to the parking lot, the tour bus we came in was long gone. It was just as well. We took a highly personalized public bus back. A kid in front of us had a big boom box and Jim Morrison was singing from it about ancient, feathered snakes. Young couples with faces shaped by Indian and Spanish blood talked loudly, laughed, smoked, and flirted. The driver had a shrine composed of the Virgin of Guadelupe, Quetzalcoatl, and some desert flowers above the dashboard. The way he was driving, he doubtlessly needed protection from as many gods as he could conjure. We barreled down the mountain from the sacred city to the living, pulsing city below.

"He's the shaman," I told Tristan. Don't know if he believed me. But he wasn't reading the books he had brought from home anymore. He wasn't listening to his tapes either. He was grooving on the sound of the boom box and he looked at the fields of corn, the slums and the burros filing by outside the window. He didn't object later on when we had some fiery chiles in a restaurant. He had no fear of the Punk Police and I swore that he snapped his fingers when some *mariachis* we didn't ask surrounded us and started playing.

Mexico, Light-Cooking
Frontier

At 5:30 A.M. on Sunday, at the intersection of Río Panuco and Río Rhin, in one of Mexico City's most elegant neighborhoods, I heard a rooster, a loud rooster, crowing in the dawn. My first thought was that, regrettably, the herald would end, before the morning was gone, in one of the many kinds of delicious soups that Mexicans consume at midday. Mexican chicken soups, as varied as the many regions of Mexico, are rich in stock, flavored with cilantro, peppers, and lime, and surprisingly light.

The night before the morning of the rooster, I had sat in the Bar La Cueva on Calle Callas, near this same intersection, and had a bowl of the local chicken soup, chased with a bottle of *light* Dos Equis. Yes, it was true! The famed Mexican beer had introduced a light variety just before my arrival. The businessmen who frequented the joint were pretty health-conscious, judging by their unusual slimness. They were eating lean strips of roasted chicken with salsas in little dishes on the side. A long buffet featured a variety of salads. Could this be the Mexico I knew and loved? Not a bowl of *menudo,* tripe soup, was to be seen.

Of course, I didn't have to go far for the Mexico that gives us calorie counters nightmares. Just outside Bar La Cueva, a popular *taquería* was frying tacos, beef, chicken, and pork, with abandon. A line of older-style businessmen with the more traditional waistlines waited outside for a turn at the crowded little place.

Surprisingly though, Mexico is a more health-conscious place these days. Vegetarian restaurants abound in Mexico City. One of my favorites, Super Soya, *El Centro Dietético y Naturista Más Completo de Mexico,* at 40 Calle de Tacuba, features a bewildering array of health products, along with a long lunch counter where busy short-order cooks prepare delicious and exotic dishes. There is the pineapple-green-pepper-spinach-papaya-potato-apple pizza, for instance, by the slice. There are a variety of soy burgers with a free salad and several condiments. Best of all, there are dozens of fruit drinks, *liquados,* made from mango, pineapple, bananas, watermelon, guava, and several fruits I didn't recognize. You can have your *liquado* with water or with milk. Being the tourist I am, I was afraid of water, so I drank my guava juice with milk. It tasted sublime, and it was cheap: about a dollar for the tall glass.

Mexico is a fruit lover's paradise. Little stands on the street sell paper cups of slices of peeled, ripe mango with lime juice for a few pennies. There are juice stands on every street. The lovely dining room at the Maria Christina Hotel on Calle Rio Lerma serves fresh fruit and fruit juices for breakfast. I much prefer this old-fashioned, laid-back hotel just outside the overpriced, tourist-conscious Zona Rosa. When the weather is good, you can eat on the patio and imagine yourself back in colonial Mexico. Along with your fresh orange juice, they will bring you *café con leche*, and thin toast wrapped in linen napkins.

Outside Mexico City, the challenge to light eating becomes more interesting. Sitting at one of the cafés on the *zócalo* in the ancient colonial city of Oaxaca, you barely need to eat at all. The fresh mountain air combines with the bright colors to give you an indescribably light feeling. When and if you finally decide to eat, you can stroll to any number of *taquerias* and regional restaurants specializing in Oaxaquena fare. Oaxaca cooking is fiery and rich. Or you can do as I did: walk to the market near the *zócalo* and buy fresh bread, *queso*—the local stringy cheese, a fresh tomato and a thick scallion, a papaya, and a mango. Add a bottle of mineral water to your feast, and then buy the English-language newspaper, *Mexico City News* (the only one available), sit on a bench, and share your bread with the pigeons. Sooner or later, you will notice that some locals, as well as some travel-wise Europeans, are doing the same, seated on benches all around the plaza. Soon, the sun will set and the first musicians will begin to tune their instruments for the evening concert. After you dispose of the remains of your meal and the English-language newspaper, you settle back and let the sound of Mexican popular music, and then the strains of the military brass band, envelop you in a cocoon of dreaming. You think about poor Malcolm Lowry, who wrote his masterpiece, *Under the Volcano* at Hotel Francia here, while killing himself with tequila and mescal. You may even get up and have a mescal in his honor. It's a light-tasting but powerful drink, full of the ancient voices of Indian Mexico.

Next morning, the *zócalo* was still asleep, and the waiters at the sidewalk café of the Marquis del Valle were lazily putting on the first tablecloths. There was a chill in the air from the mountains. I ordered the simplest *desayuno*—coffee, pan tostada, fresh orange juice. It was a slight eight pesos, about two dollars. Only the pigeons and the basket vendors were awake.

One of them, a man-basket with dozens of hand-woven baskets attached to him like multicolored balloons, approached and sold me a basket. Oaxaca crafts are sophisticated and diverse. This basket was perfect for the day's picnic. I planned to repeat the trip to the market and then go to the ancient city of ruins at Monte Albán, to eat there, lightly, among the ghosts of that ancient civilization. Some of its cooking secrets were, doubtless, available to the attentive meditator.

France *et les* Français

The French eat. And how! I went to Brittany on the French Atlantic coast a few days after the fiftieth anniversary of D-Day. I have this thing about going places a few days after something big happened. That's when you see people as they really are. The guests have gone home and the natives finally relax. *"C'est incroyable, Paupette, m'petit chou,* what bad table manners our liberators had!" I was a guest too, but at something smaller than D-Day, namely a literary conference about the Romanian avant-garde at Saint-Nazaire. The Romanian avant-garde, you may know, has given France some of its brightest moments. Along with General de Gaulle, Tristan Tzara, the founder of Dadaism, is one of France's most arrogant personages.

The conference took place in a hotel right on the beach. From the restaurant, which was the true heart of the event, one could see topless bathers, turning slowly on the spit of the bright noon sun. The four-course lunch might begin with two shrimp-filled avocados, followed by a local fish in a lemony bérnaise with white rice and white wine, followed by thick slices of Camembert and red wine, topped by a fresh strawberry tart and black coffee. At this lunch one could, if one wished, position one's fork and knife to chart the course of one of the roasting beauties on the beach. Dinner might begin with a light cauliflower cream soup, followed by salmon on a bed of mushrooms with sautéed onions, rare lamb fillets with french fries, gruyère, pastry, white and red wines, coffee and brandies. At this dinner one could watch the sun set over the coast of Brittany and reflect, if one wished, on the pleasures of civilization and shiver at the thought that only fifty years ago Nazis bunked in this hotel and their machine-gun nests took the place of top-less bathers.

The city of Saint-Nazaire on the French Atlantic coast was rebuilt after the war in a style someone called American: wide boulevards that intersect at straight angles. "America," this someone also said, pointing to the ocean, "is right over there, directly across." On the beach, there is a monument to the American liberators of France. It would seem that America is big with the natives. But then, someone else, speaking of the same town, said: "Saint-Nazaire always had wide, straight boulevards, because it was built by Napoleon. It was rebuilt after the Napoleonic, not the American style." And on second look, there really is nothing American about it: the central park is flanked by patisseries, cafés, and official buildings. Over the quaint waterfront, a poetic sign proclaims the glory of the lights at night over the harbor. The Catholic church dominates the landscape: a traditional wedding is in progress, the bride festooned with local flowers and embroidery.

The town's third biggest industry after the port and tourism is culture. The town's mayor hands out proclamations to poets. And in discussions about America, people seem to hold the most extraordinary opinions. "America is going to implode," someone assures me, "from all the pressures of the minorities." I assure him that America is not going to do anything of the sort. "It is a place where laws and morality have broken up," says someone else. Once again, I make the case that, quite the contrary, it is the upholding of the laws that keeps America on course. "It is the world's biggest power and look how weak it acts," shouts another. This, unfortunately, is something I agree with, but I find myself arguing nonetheless. There is something about the French criticizing America that brings out the demon in me.

After a couple of hours of this, I'm ready for a walk on the beach. There it is, the monument to the liberators of France. Kvetch all you want, I think, and then I see a big graffito on a wall: VIVE LA RÉPUBLIQUE SOCIALISTE BRETONNE! Of course. This is Brittany. They don't even like the French here: they have their own separatist movement. Delusion is general, only irony is forever.

After a few days of speaking French and Romanian at this literary conference in France, I started to lose my mind. I couldn't remember simple English words like *of* and *which.* By the end of the week, I had a complete linguistic nervous breakdown. I sat down at a café amid miniskirts and maxiprices, and ate a crepe, trying to remember how to say, "This is weird." My whole face had been rearranged by Latin sounds and I was unable to recall the language I had spent thirty years and several lives in. I felt like a soap opera amnesiac who goes out for croissants one morning and next minute he's forgotten his name and his address. Only this was worse. It was psychosis.

My forgotten first language, Romanian, rose to the surface like a submerged continent, dragging with it early memories, sweeping English like sand out of the way. I tried to recover. I bought an English newspaper and practiced some automatic writing on the café napkin. But the British paper alienated me further. British was not American: it was something continental, rooted in the European Atlantic. And my automatic writing turned up in Latin syntax.

I had experienced something like this once before, on a smaller scale. After a week-long visit by my mother, with whom I speak Romanian, I heard everyone speaking Romanian in my mother's voice. On the streets, on buses, in restaurants, hundreds of men and women spoke to each other in Romanian in my mother's voice. I told myself that they couldn't possibly be speaking Romanian, because I couldn't understand a word they said. But this bit of logic did not alleviate the condition. I kept hearing this way until the sound faded. But now something even graver was happening: I was about to be returned to my native tongue and its linguistic cousin, French, without recourse to either logic or English voices. Obviously, I'm better now since I'm writing this in American, but I think a psycholinguist should look into this. It might be a window into the madness of millions.

Jerusalem

On a ledge overlooking the Wailing Wall, a group of religious Jews sit silently in the rain behind a banner proclaiming the imminent arrival of the Messiah. They shouldn't bother: the Messiah, when He comes, won't be coming to Jerusalem. He'll go directly to CNN headquarters in Atlanta. Jerusalem is too complicated.

At Yad Vashem, the Holocaust Museum, in a room full of an infinity of lights, voices read without surcease the names of the million and a half children murdered by the Nazis. It's unbearable, one name after another, some familiar, some strange, and their ages. That's all. My friend Benny Hendel, who is one of the voices reading these names, took me here first. This is Israel, a place for the Jews, he said by this gesture.

At the Wailing Wall, the metal detectors let the worshippers in one by one. Men to the left, women to the right. The pilgrims lay their foreheads on the cold stone, its cracks filled with myriad prayers on tightly rolled paper strips.

Beyond the Wall, the Dome of the Rock, covered in gold, glitters with Mohammed's dream of heaven.

At the holiest site of Christendom, the grave of Jesus Christ and the site of His crucifixion, an ancient Copt weeps into his Bible. An Australian woman on her knees kisses the myrrh-scented stone where His body was prepared for burial. A Japanese tourist snaps pictures.

In the Old City, where only the occasional tourist ventures now, young Arab boys move quickly between the narrow stalls groaning with unsold saffron and fragrant oils. On top of the Damascus Gate an Israeli soldier with a machine gun carefully watches them.

On the Via Dolorosa a mule laden with gasoline cans ascends the hill past the graves of Jewish kings and prophets, past the Byzantine churches, the Crusader forts, and the mosques, led by an old man wrapped in his *kaffiyeh*. And on the horizon, beyond the layered graves of four thousand years, shines the white harmonica of the new Mormon Temple. And beyond that, like fine hairs etched on the sky over the Mount of Olives, stand construction cranes, at work on new subdivisions.

And in this palimpsest of graves and stone, everyone waits for the Messiah to come, a political solution, or just a major miracle. While waiting, there is a great vegetarian restaurant on Emek Efraim Street with hip, punk-do'ed waitresses who speak, like everyone else, six languages. And next door is a bakery and a movie theater, and just past the walled-in, barbed-wired, abandoned cemetery of the German Templars is a great café and nightclub.

The Messiah, in my opinion, would find this place confusing, but it's heaven for the philosopher.

Israel, Country of Talk

I srael is a country of talk. My friend Benny Hendel, who works for Israeli radio, could've been me. Or I him. We both left Romania about the same time: he went to Israel, I came to America. We both remember Christmas in Romania when we got oranges from Haifa, wrapped in crinkly tissue paper with mysterious black Hebrew letters on them. There was something dangerous and forbidden about that script, which is why I am amazed to see so much of it: Hebrew letters on billboards, advertisements, gas stations, even manhole covers. So much text in my once-secret language is matched only by the streams of multilingual talk on the streets. I hear Hebrew, Russian, Romanian, Arabic, Hungarian, English, Ethiopian, German, and French within half an hour.

And everyone is loud, emphatic, seemingly arguing. An elderly woman and a small grocery owner shout at each other. "What are they fighting about?" I ask Benny. Benny said, "They are not. She said: 'Do you have any tomatoes?' and he said, 'What, I look like I don't have any tomatoes?' " *They* may not be fighting, but everyone else is. On the subject of Arabs you cannot converse rationally with my cousin, for instance. According to her, every one of them carries a knife. They are treacherous, sneaky liars, and Jews can't have peace with them. It's racism, much as she denies it. At the other end are Benny's friends, people like the writer David Grossman who wrote *Sleeping on a Wire: Conversations with Palestinians in Israel.* His book, a book of voices, is an intelligent and furious geyser of talk rising and falling impotently while the *intifada* was raging. Since he wrote the book, things have gotten worse. Benny's dinner guests, including David, couldn't remember the last time they've been to the Old City, the Arab Quarter, where they used to play as children. I get the impression from them that now is a time of action and they are all tired of talk. Yet hopelessly entangled as things are here, talk is the only way, and on they go, voices in every language.

They Did It in Pastels

St. Petersburg, Florida, is what happens when you take out a box of pastels and paint in the sky, the houses, the bushes, and the people. Gold turned into pink then lavender then velvety blue over the Gulf of Mexico while evening-gowned, golf-course-tanned folks sailed past me barely spilling a drop of their martinis or upsetting the cherry in the blue glass. I was holding on to my end of a toothpicked green olive when I heard the news that Yitzhak Rabin had been assassinated. Did anybody know? There wasn't a ripple in the crowd.

I appointed myself bad-news bear and went around informing the local oligarchy. Some knew, some didn't, but I didn't very much upset anyone until I told the Russian poet Yevgeny Yevtushenko, who made a huge, hurt noise and demanded to be led to a television set to watch the breaking news. He and I and a friend of his plunked down in front of the mega-TV and flipped channels looking for the expected coverage, but we hit only sports and old movies, and every time we ran into another football game or old movie, Yevtushenko exclaimed in frustration: "This is fascism!" And by that, he meant the extraordinary blitheness of TV at such a historic moment. Finally, we got to CNN and they were, of course, talking about it, but still they were running the sports scores at the bottom of the screen.

The Russian poet shook his head in disbelief. He had once been the first in the now nearly forgotten days of Communism to brand the specter of Russian anti-Semitism in his famous poem "Babii Yar." Now, here he sat, under the Don-Cesare-Pink sky of Florida, in the middle of a cocktail party, alone, or nearly alone, with the big bad world. He suffered the news of Rabin's murder with an intensity that made his blue eyes deeper than the pastels around us.

"I must write about this!" he exclaimed, and I think that he meant everything: the passing of a peacemaker he admired, the indifference or seeming indifference of those around him, the unperturbed inanity of television. He was far from Russia, Yevtushenko, and even farther from that Soviet Union where he had once been as famous a man as the dead prime minister.

A Few **Words** About

Christmas

I was born a Jew and raised a Communist, so what am I doing writing about Christmas?

Well, the truth is that I was never a very good Communist, and I was the kind of Jew that grew up loving Christmas. I was born in the Carpathian mountains of Romania, in an ancient German town called Sibiu, or Hermanstadt. It snowed almost as much in my town as it did in a Dickens story. The Communist authorities had banned Christmas, which they had renamed "the winter holidays," but no one paid any attention to the ban. Weeks before Christmas, the old medieval houses of my burg spruced up and began sporting wreaths, decorations, and twinkling lights. Walking through the paths carved in waist-high snow in the evenings you could see Christmas trees in every window. The smell of strudels, walnut pies, and roasts began wafting from behind the tall walls where German *Fraus* could be heard singing as they cooked.

Miraculously, oranges appeared in the usually threadbare shops. Every day, from the first of December onwards, my mother discussed with our neighbors the burning question of oranges. There were rumors as to when exactly they were supposed to arrive. I stood in line for bread and milk every morning at six A.M., before going to school, and listened carefully for hints about the oranges. Someone had it on good authority from the cousin of someone married to a man in the railroad administration that the oranges were due in the shops two days hence, on the fourteenth. A similarly authoritative source, on the other hand, claimed to have word of the oranges being sighted in a warehouse just outside of town. After many days of such agitation, the oranges finally made their brilliant, sudden, wondrous appearance in the windows of shops, which were soon mobbed until the last one vanished. The Christmas oranges, to the credit of their purveyors, were not just common oranges. They were huge, thick-skinned, individually wrapped Haifa oranges, imported from Israel. In our bleak world, dominated by the dull grays of necessity and a general air of decay and moroseness, these bright globes of sunshine were concentrated spheres of hope. They changed our mood. We became suddenly better, kinder, sweeter. It felt almost like a sin to actually *eat* these harbingers of good news. When my mother and I finally sat down with our oranges on Christmas day, we peeled them slowly, kissed the plump slices before we actually bit them, closed our eyes and, as the heavenly juice sprayed our palate, we fancied that we were cured of everything that ailed us. (The curative powers of oranges were whispered about in awe in my home town: a single orange was said to bring a dead man to life.)

Oranges from Israel were all I knew about Christmas until my mother married a Romanian railroad engineer named Puiu, who was an Orthodox Christian. I was about ten years old then, and not in the mood for a stepfather. Especially one of Puiu's generally bad temper, sour disposition, and plain nastiness. I did my best to respond in kind, so my poor mother just didn't know what to do with us. We were constantly feuding. But all that changed, quite suddenly, around Christmastime. I had seen Puiu in my room (which was only a closet between the kitchen and their bedroom, but *mine*). I asked him sharply what he thought that he was doing there without a passport. He didn't answer, so I chalked up one more offense on my ever-growing list. That night I went to sleep in a very bad mood, and tossed and turned until the tenth and final ver-

sion of my Nobel acceptance speech (most of which I spent excoriating
the despicable Puiu) worked its magic and took me out of the world. In
the middle of the night, something startled me awake. I opened my eyes
and saw that my whole room was full of soft, colored snowflakes that
twinkled everywhere. There were blue, red, gold, green flakes everywhere I looked. I then saw that each flake had *wings!* The soft, twinkling lights were angels. They made a soft music as they flew about the
room, and I was flooded with a feeling of such joy and peace I lifted off
my bed and flew between their sparkling bodies for what seemed like
a long time. I then fell asleep again. When I awoke in the morning, still
full in my bones with the good feeling of the tiny angels, I saw a Christmas tree at the foot of my bed. It was full of sparkling gold, orange, green,
and red lights. There were soft silver globes in it, and chimes that made
soft music. Under it, there were packages tied with ribbon. Unbeknownst to me, Puiu had erected this wonder while I slept.

We had a classic Christmas that year, with Puiu's relatives from near
Bucharest, some of my mother's friends, and our Hungarian next-door
neighbors. We ate a roasted goose, ham from a pig that Puiu's family
had raised all year just for this Christmas feast, and presents. I un-
wrapped mine first. It was an orange! After dinner, everyone sang songs
until their heads fell on the table and they started snoring. I stayed
awake as long as I could, and when I finally went to sleep it was looking at my tree. The tiny, lit angels came back and I floated with them.

One Christmas, when I was in elementary school, I went to my friend
Ion's village in the high mountains. The village of Rǎşinari, perched on
the steep Carpathian crags, looked as if it had stepped whole from an
illustrated book of fairy tales. The snow was very high, but there were
narrow paths leading from house to house. In the courtyard of Ion's
house, dozens of members of his family dressed in holiday cottons and
embroidered sheepskins, had gathered to watch the village butcher kill
the Christmas pig. It should have been a gory scene, but somehow it
wasn't. This pig, a fat, little mountain of ham, had been carefully fattened all year for this moment. Custom called for the roasted tail, which
was said to be the best part, to be awarded to the youngest child. Since
Ion and I were the same age, and there was no one younger, we ended
up wrestling for the delicacy. I won and, amid the general approval of
Ion's tribe, I crunched down on the smoky and crisp tail. It tasted delicious. That evening, together with the village children we went carol-
ing. We carried colorful pennants and stood before the snow-covered,
wooden peasant houses, singing Christmas songs. The people inside

showered us with candy, plaited breads, cakes, and small, hand-carved, wooden toys.

In Romania, Christmas was officially called "the winter holidays" until 1989. That Christmas, the Communist dictator Ceauşescu was executed, and Christmas became Christmas again. I was fortunate enough to be there two days after this most memorable and historical Christmas, and I was privileged to hear the bells of churches, silent for forty years of Communism, ring again.

There is something universally moving about the Christmas of everyone's childhood, no matter how painful or how privileged the rest of that childhood was. Perhaps children resemble one another more than they resemble the adults they will eventually become. The ability to experience magic is diminished in adults. It is occasionally rekindled by the memory of an occasion, particularly Christmas. I have read a variety of Christmas stories and found them to be, for the most part, about the stubborn survival of childhood magic. One is immediately transported upon hearing the bells of Dylan Thomas's "A Child's Christmas in Wales." We begin to resonate in tune with that black-and-white world of bells, "over the frozen foam of the powder and ice-cream hills, / over the crackling sea." A lovely window opens onto a bittersweet past in Clarence Major's story "Ten Pecan Pies," where the battles of a lifetime come to be played, and reconciled, over some bags of pecans. It's Depression time in America, the favorite moral ground of those who'd point to the triumph of the human spirit over material lack, and the protagonists of Laura Ingalls Wilder's "Merry Christmas" are desperately poor, so poor that they must burn hay to keep warm. In spite of everything, they manage to have a postcard Christmas. The Depression Christmases of Major and Wilder seem far removed from the upper-class Christmas that M. F. K. Fisher flees in her youth, only to return to it in middle age. And yet, in spite of their differences, the people in these stories all pursue the same goal: a need to share, to love, to end isolation.

James Thurber's gentle satire of the American mania for Christmas cards points to the not-so-gentle truth that this national deluge of friendliness may be concealing the guilt we feel about our busy lives, too busy to make time for family and friends. Another satire, "Christmas Is a Sad Season for the Poor," by John Cheever, traces the full pathos of a Sutton Place elevator man's fall from loneliness into overconcern at Christmas time. He ends up being fired, but not before he's overstuffed and loaded down with presents he has no need for, and keeps passing down the line in a grotesque parody of the "trickle-down" economy of the Republicans.

There may be great distance in both space and time between Dostoyevski's touching account of Christmas in a Siberian labor camp and Bret Harte's epic tale of sacrifice from the days of California's gold rush, but the same human heart beats insistently in both places.

Christmas in places without snow seems incongrous, unnatural. I remember missing, after I moved to California, the bracing energy of Christmas on the East Coast, particularly in New York. The throngs of shoppers in midtown, the first snow . . . these seemed as far removed from the swaying palms of Dolores Street in San Francisco as my childhood. In Peter Matthiessen's "The Cloud Forest," sailors aboard a ship in the tropics end up re-creating Christmas entirely out of their sentiments, fiercely ignoring the "brilliant macaws" and the "enormous white flowers." But if snow is what one craves, there is no snow like the snow in the stories of the master of Christmas stories, Charles Dickens. There is so much snow in "The Holly-Tree" that "we came within a town, and found the church clocks all stopped, the dial-faces choked with snow, and the inn-signs blotted out."

The narrator of Dickens's "The Holly-Tree" spends a lonely Christmas snowed in at an inn, and passes the time remembering all the inns he has known in his life. The memories of these places, with their people and ghosts, spring to life, making the air livelier than if a loud party had been in progress. This is a grown-up's Christmas, which unlike a child's, is more full of memories than of laughter.

In the end, Christmas divides in two like Gaul: the children's Christmas, with its ever-present intensity, and the grown-ups', with its inevitable sadness. Both Christmases are amply evidenced by the literature. Reading these stories was just a job in the beginning, but in the end I realized that I had quite a bit more Christmas in me than I had anticipated given my original circumstances.

The **Torah** from Sibiu

At the end of World War II, American GIs in Europe discovered a warehouse full of Jewish religious objects. They had been looted by the Nazis from the synagogues of Eastern Europe, and were being stored for an eventual "Museum of the Jews." The Nazis were going to build it when they had murdered all the Jews. Among these objects was the Torah from the synagogue in Sibiu, my hometown in Romania. The Torah, the sacred scroll on which the Bible is written, is said to contain all the souls of the people living in the community. If so, surely, the souls of my grandfather and grandmother and those of their mothers and fathers and many before them, were contained within.

After the war, American Jewish congregations adopted many of the orphaned Torahs. The Sibiu Torah ended up in Dallas, Texas, at the Shalom Synagogue. On February 9, Rabbi Kenneth Roseman of the Shalom temple, invited me to help rededicate the Torah of Sibiu.

The rabbi gave me an affectionate tour of his modern reform temple, an architecturally daring place full of light and hope, which he had helped design. He was clearly proud of this American building, with its active congregation, cultural activities, and school.

But when he removed the ancient Torah from Sibiu from the cabinet in the chapel, time stood still. He removed the frayed velvet cover with its embroidered lettering and set it gently down. An ancient scribe had written the Hebrew letters of the sacred text in a beautiful hand. I touched the wood handles and felt the souls of my ancestors close in.

"We give this Torah to children to hold," the rabbi said. "That way each one of them becomes responsible for the soul of one Jew from Sibiu."

The first Jews came to Sibiu in the fourteenth century. They were decimated by pogroms, wars, and dictatorships. And yet here are American children, caretaking their tortured European souls. Surely, that's a triumph of love over time.

But the story isn't over, not even in America.

Not long ago, Dallas nazis sprayed swastikas on the Shalom Synagogue, and threatened to bomb it.

Yes, Mother

Three weeks before I came to visit, mother went shopping. She bought three plastic bags full of shredded lettuce for the salad, one chicken for the chicken with dumplings, twenty squashes for the stuffed-cabbage-style stuffed squash dish, five containers of cottage cheese, three pounds of cream cheese, and a quart of whipped cream for the crepes, and three gallons of sour cream to go on top of the chicken and the squash. Ten days before I actually arrived, mother deboned the chicken, boiled the rice, split open the squashes, and ripped up the lettuce bags. Five days before countdown, she boiled the chicken, julienned and steamed the squash, threw the lettuce into a wooden bowl, stirred the sour cream in a big glass jar, and went shopping again. This time she got nine green peppers, five bunches of red radishes, six flat noodle packages, and all new wineglasses. During the remaining hours she stuffed the squashes, buried the chicken in dumplings, rolled the crepes, and stirred vigorously the sour cream, which, if left alone, tends to lump. Nine hours before my plane landed, mother fired up the burners and the oven and set the various mini-mountains of food on them and in it. One hour before landing, while the plane was still in the air, mother was on the phone with her advisers. She had forgotten the dill, which goes into the stuffed squash if the squash is going to turn out. The details of the last-minute dill hunt are hazy now, but they involved extraordinary fits of driving, running, grabbing, chopping, seasoning, and reinserting. This last-minute dash for dill was detrimental to the hair done so well by the hairdressers the day before in the interstices between chopping and boiling and now a retouch was in order. Too late.

The door opened and the prodigal son walked in. With bits of crepe caught in her bangs and shredded dill filling the air like an escaped licorice demon, mother said, "Are you hungry?," and I responded, as I used to when I was a boy and came home starving, "Yes, I am." The only difference was that when I was a boy who came home starving there was nothing to eat because my mother didn't cook. She was a working woman who didn't have time and didn't know how. A succession of maids fed us: a young Hungarian girl who fed us sour-cream topped stuffed cabbage, an ancient Transylvanian crone who burned onions into chicken flesh, a decommissioned army cook who pounded squash with rice into a thin tomato sauce. I hated them all and when we didn't have cooks because we didn't have any money, mother and I ate bread with plum jam. And that was perfectly okay.

I sat down at the table and one by one imitations of the dishes I hated in my childhood appeared like bad dreams from my mother's over-wrought American kitchen. I slathered on the sour cream and grinned with crooked delight. The next day, we gave the leftovers to the Polish people next door. They were nostalgic for Central European cooking. We had rye bread with jam, mother and I.

Time, Merciless Beast

Time is a merciless beast, as my mother would say. It devours the unweary and it grounds the mighty. Here it is, fall again, but instead of feeling like a new school kid happy to kick leaves on my way to meeting the new girl with the ponytail, I stand before a mountain of paper and cry. They want me to do things, type things, speak things, pass judgments and compose opinions, but all I'm good for is dribbling the basketball of memory on the hard cement of reality.

The Man Who Was Always One Day Late

I was sitting at the Capitol Hotel bar in Little Rock, Arkansas, staring out the window. A baffled tourist across the street was looking both ways to see where the action was. There wasn't any. Little Rock was as sleepy this afternoon as Juarez after lunch. He was one day late.

The day before fifteen thousand Razorback fans had taken to the streets to celebrate the team's victory in the Final Four. In front of the Rose Law Firm, Operation Rescue conducted some incomprehensible pickets. "Randall Terry must be running for President," someone guessed, "and he's starting by running against Hillary!" I see. That's a preborn kinda strategy. But it's an abortion, if you ask me.

Anyway, there it was, all this action and the baffled tourist had missed it. I recognized him. This tourist was no other than The Man Who Is Always One Day Too Late. You see this guy in New Orleans, the day after Mardi Gras. In Washington, the morning after the cherry blossoms fall off. In San Francisco, after the Gay Pride parade. In Moscow, after the coup.

I know this guy because I'm not him. I'm always right there. If I'm going somewhere, stuff happens. You can say I'm the advance for this guy who gets there late. I telegraph, phone, fax him: Come, I say, it's happening now! But I always miss him by a minute. And then it's a minute too late.

This is a man who intends well, mind you. But history doesn't like him. I also know a guy who doesn't want to be there when things are happening. At Mardi Gras, he leaves town. If there is any excitement wherever he is, he flees by the nearest conveyance. This is The Man Who Is Never There on Purpose. He despises history.

Sometimes the three of us have lunch: The Man Who Is Always One Day Too Late, The Man Who Is Always Right There, and The Man Who Doesn't Want to Be There. We discuss our condition. I'm the only one who gets to eat. Because I'm the only one there.

Our Daily **Noise**

At midnight, the trees were un-plugged and the cicadas fell silent. The frogs quit their love-sick cho-rus about one A.M. At three A.M. the drunks began cursing their way home in the dark. At four A.M., somebody's car alarm went off. It screeched anxiously the rest of the night. Now and then the low, mourn-ful moans of barges pulling chemicals down the Mississippi River in-tervened to temper the hysterical car. At five A.M., the car was joined by a distressed house that began howling for help in a strangled voice like a mezzo-soprano being choked. Twenty minutes later there was the sound of broken glass and two voices raised in anger. Stella and Stan-ley were at it again. Eeeee! went Stella. Ugh! Ugh! Ugh! went Stanley. Well, that was just enough to get the birds started. Normally polite until six A.M., the birds of New Orleans don't just wake up: they explode up.

First to join in was a mockingbird with a vast repertoire that includes car alarms, slamming car doors, house doors and alarms, ringing telephones, domestic squabbles, and river barges. Like a digest mirror of all that shakes in the night, this bird and its acolytes, who all belong I believe to the Mockingbird School of Mirroring Sorry Humanity, begin to throw up everything that we have done to ourselves during the night. Once the mockers are up, all hell breaks loose in the trees and every bird that thinks it has something to say starts chattering. After that, it's the sound of swearing at the new day, showers starting, coffeepots whistling, drunks collapsing, more phones ringing, and Stanley and Stella moaning like two house alarms with dying batteries. I'm not saying that the New Orleans night is louder than, let's say, the New York night, but the tropical sound gumbo is pretty unique. And whoever does sleep dreams loud and in color. Ayayai!

Animals Under Attack

It's springtime and animals are under attack. You would think that spring, when humans are most like animals, would be the very season to give animals special consideration. But no. The sturgeon, a venerable dinosaur-age holdout, is about to disappear. The flood-control dams in waterways from the Missouri to the Yellowstone River have finally done them in. Only a few thousand of these ancient beings remain. Meanwhile, in the labs there is talk of cloning cows without brains so that we can eat meat without remorse. These brainless cows, the wisdom goes, will not suffer when they die so we won't have to feel bad. Why grow the whole cow? I ask you. Grow just the rump roast. Or the tripe. Picasso really *was* a genius: he abstracted the cow until only its outline remained. He must have been seeing far into the labs of the future.

Even the images of animals are under attack: the much-maligned bat is now being sold at Easter in chocolate form. The manufacturers claim that it's to save them from their blood-sucking image. I think it's so that we can torture, manhandle, and cute them to death every Easter just like rabbits.

Movies have long mistreated animals both in life and in their image, but now, it turns out, movie animals are disrupting cities. In Des Moines, Iowa, downtown business ground to a halt when huge sci-fi slugs were filmed attacking JC Penney. I have nothing against real animals attacking downtown Des Moines, but movie animals only make people meaner to real animals. The animal world is, unfortunately, incapable of a sustained defense. Here and there, a bear will ravage a medicine cabinet. A herd of deer will eat some grapes. A weasel will commit suicide in a drainpipe. A stray wolf will eat a sheep. An alligator will snatch a student sleeping by the bayou. A mosquito will pierce the Off! defense. A spider will cause swelling. It isn't much. Only the animals in us can defend the animals out there. It's spring. Let's feel for all creatures without offices in Washington.

Toward a Godlike Body

The TV sold me a Solo-Flex over the holidays. I have been quietly wishing for a godlike body ever since the last time I watched TV and noticed some perfect humans doing acrobatic things. The Solo-Flex, they said, will give you this godlike body if you follow the three-times-a-week exercise without fail. It didn't say for how long. On the demo tape, the person who demo'd had a godlike body to begin with so I had no idea what he started with. What I had to start with was a tiny—I swear—potbelly caused by the food-rich city of New Orleans, biceps exercised only by lifting books, thighs used to climbing aboard buses and airplanes, and one typing finger on the verge of carpal tunnel syndrome. Once these insufficiently trained areas were corrected, my godlike body would follow.

After two weeks, a huge truck stopped in front of the house and a tiny man asked me to help him unload the thing. I grabbed one end and fell down. "You sure need this thing," said the tiny man, disgusted. I could only help him to the hallway.

The Solo-Flex, like most things these days, was a collection of thousands of pieces of metal and rubber bands. I stood before it the way a reader of novels in the nineteenth century might stand before interactive hypertext. With the help of my son, who has inherited a fragmented world and therefore has no trouble putting it back together, we knocked the Solo-Flex together. I then studied the chart.

Every other day six different sets of exercises, twelve repetitions of each, were necessary for the godlike body. Each exercise involved another arrangement of the Solo-Flex, which had to be taken completely apart and reconfigured for that exercise. With great difficulty I created the first configuration, a strange rubber-banded bed on which I lay. And lay. I could do the lift maybe once. But not twelve times three times. It's been two weeks. My godlike body waits for me in the Solo-Flex, but I've been going in the back door to avoid it. I think I'll just carry more books until I'm ready.

Insomnia

There it was, by God, the thought that everything was wrong. It was wrong, it was broken. It was way past being fixed. It could have, at one time, but I'd let it go. I'd created it, innocently enough, it is true, but I had let it go on and on and now it was too late. It was too late for it, for me, for everyone involved, it was just damn, plain late. I looked at the bedside clock, a loud, luminous, gassy assertion of numbers. One-thirty A.M. It would get later still. I knew that between the first time I looked at it and the second time the numbers would have grown brighter, louder, more awake, and it would be later still. Two. Two-Ten. Two-Forty. Three. Three-Three. My favorite digital moment in the unending sweat of logic that wouldn't break down.

Three-Three, the portal to the Hour of the Wolf: Four. Four A.M., the Hour of the Wolf, is the insomniac's fork in the road.

Here, he must choose whether to go on trying to break down the thin but resilient film of argumentation with his self, or whether he ought to rise and join the world of the semiliving. It's not a bad time in the real world. Some bartenders, waiters, drunks, and college students are just heading home. Street sweepers are getting their machines warm. Newsboys are hurling the world on your doorstep. The edge of day is nearly over the Atlantic. Best of all, the over-worried *its* of the night have retreated to the backwater of the mind, temporarily beaten by their own weary circularity, and by the texture of real things. Coffee maker. Colin Powell. Toilet paper. New novel. ATC commentary. Even the numinous and anguished clock has shrunk. Still, tiredness lines every gesture like lead. My lost sleep is being slept by someone somewhere, someone innocent and at peace, someone whose thoughts aren't broken by their insoluble sorrow, someone young and untroubled who acts before thinking and sleeps when he closes his eyes. Alas. That someone was me once and that's why, doubtless, we are in trouble now.

The **Animals**, Revisited

Whenever animals are in the news it's usually something bad for them. Here in Louisiana, squads of assassins were stalking the swamp to kill the nutria rats who are eating the state, when the flood came. The nutria got a reprieve but now the night scopes are back on the guns and you can hear the *pop-pop* as the fur flies. Nutria aren't good for much: they taste like they look and their coats haven't caught on. There is talk of turning their bones into casino chips, but there is such a surplus of human bones the rats will just have to wait.

In the Grand Canyon National Park in Arizona, rangers have been killing mule deer who've become hooked on junk food left over by tourists. Doesn't make sense. Shouldn't they shoot the tourists instead?

I mean, these tourists will go on leaving half-eaten cow fragments for half-starved animals wherever they go, hooking more and more of them until there'll be lines of animals outside McDonald's like junkies outside drugstores in England.

Nutria and deer are being eliminated because they inconvenience humans, but at least somebody's standing up for fish. Wildlife and Fishery agents here busted some of Louisiana's best chefs in a surprise sting operation. It was a scene that would make a shark smile. They dragged the chefs out of their kitchens, cuffed them, and drove them downtown. Chef Apuzzo, author of two cookbooks, said while being frisked: "It's very unusual." And Chef Imbraguglio quipped as he was being cuffed: "I'm scared to death." The chefs' crime was buying protected redfish from peddlers.

The mayor of Friendsville, Maryland, meanwhile, has been exposing himself in public and getting reelected, which goes to show that animals will keep showing up in the news even after we get rid of them.

The Gator God

We've been flying the flag at half-mast here at the headquarters of the Reptile Defense League. They've killed the Gator God in South Florida. The Gator God was tracked down to a hole in the Blackwater River State Forest by a man named Godwin who'd lost his five-thousand-dollar hunting dog, Flojo. Godwin tracked Flojo's electronic collar to a hole in the swamp. Another hunter, tracking the signal of another lost hunting dog, tracked him to the same hole. The faint beeps of the lost pooches came from the belly of a twelve-foot alligator, fifty years old, who'd been feeding on pricey canines for years. When Godwin and his men slit open his belly—after a fierce struggle— they found forty collars in him. Looking on the carcass of the *dei*cided beast, a slightly chilled Godwin exclaimed: "Their bark was his dinner bell!"

There aren't many places in the world where great beasts reside. A sad bear might maul a barbecue. A snake might pierce an ankle. But no hawk will topple a TV tower. No birds will *really* terrify California. There is no Nessie in the Loch. The Gator God might be the last of the great animals: a defender of the hunted who relished the taste of the hunters.

Godwin wondered too at the proximity of his children, who had been swimming but a mile from this gator. "I guess as long as we fed him five-thousand-dollar Walker fox hunters, he wasn't about to eat the kids."

That's exactly right. He was a kind Gator God who took the sacrifices in the spirit in which they were offered. And because of him, foxes went free. And the swamp was empowered.

My friend Wood came down from Little Rock while we were mourning the Gator God and invited us all to a wedding in the bayou country, a big *fais-do-do*. "They're cooking a fifteen-foot alligator," he told, "the granddaddy of them all. Been living in my cousin's bayou for seventy-five years."

Our sorrow was redoubled now, but we secured the RDF pirogue to a cypress and piled in his car. We passed the bourbon and screamed our new motto to every passing car: YOUR BARK IS OUR DINNER BELL! YOUR BARK IS OUR DINNER BELL!

Tonight we were going to eat God.

On **Disposition** of Body **Postmortem**

(Anima Gladis)

It would be nice to belong to one of those carnal religions like Christianity, which indulges in voluptuaries. I say *nice* because Carnival, the farewell to the flesh, makes so much of extracting music from *carne* every New Orleans festival season. The afterlife industry, thanks to Anne Rice and the Catholic-Voodoo Church, is also situated in New Orleans. So, I dig it, as they say, but for my own *corpus* I prefer its afterlife to be literary. I edit *The Exquisite Corpse: A Journal of Letters & Life,* which is an offering of literature in lieu of my actual body, which I intend to keep as long as it stays rigorous. As for the actual disposition of putrid meat postmortem, I prefer that it be incinerated lest it end up in a nouveau-Baudelairean poem. One *charogne* is enough. The ashes may, of course, be respectfully collected in a silver urn that ought to be polished by the collector with lemon juice every year or so. For monuments, I would like a bronze plaque of the sort that abounds in New Orleans, placed at several addresses, bearing messages that go from one to the next so that, in the end, a fine tour of New Orleans can be had. There will be bookstalls on the way so that commerce goes on and my heirs keep profiting.

AcKnowLeDgMenTs

All the shorter essays here were first broadcast on National Public Radio's "All Things Considered." Other pieces appeared as follows: "My House in the Sky" served as an introduction to the book *Over America*, published in conjunction with the PBS television series by the same name; "Roll On, Big River!" first appeared in *Sierra*, the magazine of the Sierra Club; "Democracy on the Skin" appeared in *In-Print*, a publication of National Public Radio; "Whose Woods Are These?" was originally written for a conference at the Humphrey Institute in Minneapolis; versions of it appeared later in *The Nation* and *Reframing America*, a photography book on immigrants published by the Tucson Center for Creative Photography; "Am Myth: Whazzit, Whozzit, Whozinonit?" was written for a panel at the American Conservatory Theatre in San Francisco on the subject: Is There a Common Mythic Theme in American Culture?, and later published in the *City Lights Review*; "A Report on the State of Revolution(s) for Rosa Luxemburg" was written for the Rosa Luxemburg Conference at Chicago's Blue Rider Theater, and published in *New American Writing*; "Fairy-Tale Sport Babes" and "The Talking Cure Becomes the Talking Virus" were broadcast as commentaries on ABC's *Nightline*; "Intelligent Electronics" was written for the annual conference in New Orleans of Intelligent Electronics; "Some Remarks on Interactivity" was written for a panel on Tracking the Interactive Idiom for the World Digital Conference in Los Angeles, and published in *Digital Media: A Seybold Report*; "Sex, the World" was the foreword to an anthology of international erotic writing edited by Lily Pond and Richard A. Russo; "Swimming Between Languages" was the keynote address at the NAFSA conference in New Orleans; "Brâncuşi" was written for the opening of the Constantin Brâncuşi 1995 retrospective at the Philadelphia Museum of Art; "World-Without-Walls: The Impossible Return" was written for an exhibition of stones from the Berlin Wall at the South Dakota School of Mines, and published in *Exquisite Corpse*; "Where Have All the Jokes in Eastern Europe Gone?" was a conference paper on Alternative Futures, sponsored by Grantmakers in the Arts; "Where Is the Heart of Transylvania?" was first delivered at the Unitarian Universalist Church in Arlington, Virginia, and published in *World*, the journal of the Unitarian Universalist Association; "Father and Son Undertake Search for Brujo" was published in *American Way*, the magazine of American Airlines; "Mexico, Light-Cooking Frontier" was published in *Cooking Light*, the magazine of food and fitness; "A Few Words About Christmas" was the introduction to *Christmas Stories*, Chronicle Books, San Francisco.

About the AuThoR

ANDREI CODRESCU was born in Sibiu, Romania, in 1946. Since emigrating to the United States in 1966, he has published poetry, memoirs, fiction, and essays. He is a regular commentator on National Public Radio, and wrote and starred in the award-winning movie *Road Scholar*. His novel, *The Blood Countess* (Simon & Schuster, 1995), was a national best-seller. He teaches writing at Louisiana State University in Baton Rouge, Louisiana, and edits *Exquisite Corpse: A Journal of Letters & Life*.